Memoirs Of Arthur Hamilton, B. A. Of Trinity College, Cambridge

by

Arthur Christopher Benson

Memoirs Of Arthur Hamilton, B. A. Of Trinity College, Cambridge
by Arthur Christopher Benson

ISBN: 978-93-63053-31-1

Published by

DOUBLE 9 BOOKS

2/13-B, Ansari Road
Daryaganj, New Delhi – 110002
info@double9books.com
www.double9books.com
Tel. 011-40042856

ABOUT THE AUTHOR

Arthur Christopher Benson, FRSL was an English essayist, poet, and professor who was born on April 24, 1862, and died on June 17, 1925. He was the 28th Master of Magdalene College, Cambridge. Among other things, he wrote the words to Edward Elgar's Coronation Ode and the words to the patriotic song "Land of Hope and Glory" (1902). People really liked his poems, articles, and reviews of other writers' work. He was also known for writing ghost stories. Bernard Benson was born on April 24, 1862, at Wellington College in Berkshire. He was the sixth child of Edward White Benson (1829–1896), who was the first teacher of the college and later became Archbishop of Canterbury from 1883 to 1896. His mother, Mary Sidgwick Benson, was related to the scientist Henry Sidgwick. Edward Frederic Benson, who is best known for his Mapp and Lucia books, and Robert Hugh Benson, who was a priest in the Church of England before becoming a Roman Catholic and wrote many famous books, were also brothers of Benson. Margaret Benson, their sister, was an artist, an author, and a self-taught Egyptologist.

CONTENTS

DEDICATION

To H. L. M.

My dear Friend,

When you were kind enough to allow me to dedicate this book to you you, to whose frank discussion of sacred things and kindly indifference to exaggerations of expression I owe so much—I felt you were only adding another to the long list of delicate benefits for which a friend can not be directly repaid.

My object has throughout been this: I have seen so much of what may be called the dissidence of religious thought and religious organization among those of my own generation at the Universities, and the unhappy results of such a separation, that I felt bound to contribute what I could to a settlement of this division, existing so much more in word than in fact—a point which you helped me very greatly to grasp.

I have been fortunate enough to have seen and known both sides of the battle. I have seen men in the position of teachers, both anxious and competent to position of teachers, both anxious and competent to settle differences, when brought into contact with men of serious God-seeking souls, with the nominal intention of dropping the bandying of words and cries and of attacking principles, meet and argue and part, almost unconscious that they have never touched the root of the matter at all, yet dissatisfied with the efforts which only seem to widen the breach they are intended to fill.

And why? Both sides are to blame, no doubt: the teachers, for being more anxious to expound systems than to listen to difficulties, to make their theories plain than to analyse the theories of their—I will not say adversaries—but opponents; the would-be learners, for hasty generalization; for bringing to the conflict a deliberate prejudice against all traditional authority, a want of patience in translating dogmas into life, a tendency to flatly deny that such a transmutation is possible.

Fortunately, the constructive side is in no want of an exponent; but I have tried to give a true portrait in this arrangement, or rather selection, of realities, of what a serious and thoughtful soul-history may in these days be: to depict the career of a character for which no one can fail to have the profoundest sympathy, being as it is, by the nature of its case, condemned to a sadder sterner view of life than its uprightness justifies, and deprived of the helpful encouragement of so many sweet natures, whose single aim in life is to help other souls, if they only knew how.

And so, as I said before, it is with a most grateful remembrance of certain gracious words of yours, let fall in the stately house of God where we have worshipped together, in lecture-rooms where I have sat to hear you, and in conversations held in quiet college rooms or studious gardens, that I place your name at the head of these pages, the first I have sent out to shift for themselves, or rather to pass whither the Inspirer of all earnest endeavour may appoint.

I remain ever affectionately yours,
Christopher Carr.
Ashdon, Hants.

PREFACE

There are several forms of temperament. The kind that mostly issues in biography is the practical temperament. Poets have the shortest memoirs, and the most uninteresting. The politician, the philanthropist, the general, make the best, the most graphic Lives. The fact remains, however, that the question, "What has he done?" though a specious, is an unsatisfactory test of greatness.

But there is a temperament called the Reflective, which works slowly, and with little apparent result. The very gift of expression is a practical gift: with the gift of expression the reflective man becomes a writer, a poet, an artist; without it, he is unknown.

The reflective temperament, existing without any particular gift of expression, wants an exponent in these times. Reflection is lost sight of; philanthropy is all the rage. I assert that for a man to devote himself to a reflective life, that is, in the eyes of the world, an indolent one, is often a great sacrifice, and even on that account, if not essentially, valuable. Philanthropy is generally distressing, often offensive, sometimes disastrous.

Nothing, in this predetermined world, fails of its effect, as nothing is without its cause. There is a call to reflection which a man must follow, and his life then becomes an integral link in the chain of circumstance. Any intentional life affects the world; it is only the vague drifting existences that pass it by.

The subject of this memoir was, as the world counts reputation, unknown. His only public appearance, as far as I know, besides the announcement of his birth, is the fact that his initials stand in a dedication on the title-page of a noble work of fiction.

Arthur Hamilton left me his manuscripts, papers, and letters; from these, and casual conversations I have had with him in old days, this little volume is constructed.

C.C.

CHAPTER I

He was born November 2, 1852. He was the second son of a retired cavalry officer, who lived in Hampshire. Besides his elder brother, there were three sisters, one of whom died. His father was a wealthy man, and had built himself a small country house, and planted the few acres of ground round it very skillfully. Major Hamilton was a very religious man, of the self-sufficient, puritanical, and evangelical type, that issues from discipline; a martinet in his regiment, a domestic tyrant, without intending to be. He did not marry till rather late in life; and at the time when Arthur was growing up—the time when memory intwines itself most lingeringly with its surroundings, the time which comes back to us at ecstatic moments in later, sadder days—all the *entourage* of the place was at its loveliest. Nothing ever equalled the thrill, he has told me, of finding the first thrush's nest in the laurels by the gate, or of catching the first smell of the lilac bushes in spring, or the pungent scent of the chamomile and wild celery down by the little stream.

The boy acquired a great love for Nature, though not of the intimate kind that poets have by instinct. "In moments of grief and despair," he wrote in later life, "I do not, as some do, crouch back to the bosom of the great Mother; she has, it seems, no heart for me when I am sorry, though she smiles with me when I am glad." But he has told me that he is able to enjoy a simple village scene in a way that others can not easily understand: a chestnut crowded with pink spires, the clack of a mill-wheel, the gush of a green sluice out of a mantled pool, a little stream surrounded by flags and water lobelias, gave him all his life a keen satisfaction in his happy moments. "I always gravitate to water," he writes. "I could stop and look at a little wayside stream for hours; and a pool—I never tire of it, though it awes me when I am alone."

The boy was afraid of trees, as many children are. If he had to go out alone he always crossed the fields, and never went by the wood; wandering in a wood at night was a childish nightmare of a peculiarly horrible kind.

I quote a few childish stories about him, selecting them out of a large number.

His mother saying to him one day that the gardener was dead, he burst out laughing (with that curious hysteria so common in children), and then after a little asked if they were going to bury him.

His mother, wishing to familiarize him with the idea of continued existence after death, dwelt on the fact that it was only his body that was going to be buried: his soul was in heaven.

The boy said presently, "If his body is in the churchyard, and his soul in heaven, where is David?"

Upon which his mother sent him down to the farm.

He was often singularly old-fashioned in his ways. If he was kept indoors by a childish ailment, he would draw his chair up to the fire, by his nurse, and say, "Now that the children are gone out, nurse, we can have a quiet talk." And he always returned first of all his brothers and sisters, if they were playing in the garden, that he might have the pleasure of clapping his hands from the nursery window to summon them in. "Children, children, come in," he used to say.

A curious little dialogue is preserved by his aunt in a diary. He laughed so immoderately at something that was said at lunch by one of his elders, that when his father inquired what the joke was, he was unable to answer. "It must be something very funny," said his mother in explanation. "Arthur never laughs unless there is a joke." The little boy became grave at once, and said severely, "There's hardly ever anything to laugh at in what you say; but I always laugh for fear people should be disappointed."

He was very sensitive to rebuke. "I am not so sensitive as I am always supposed to be," he said to me once. "I am one of those people who cry when they are spoken to, and do it again."

For instance, he told me that, being very fond of music when he was small, he stole down one morning at six to play the piano. His father, a very early riser, was disturbed by the gentle tinkling, and coming out of his study, asked him rather sharply why he couldn't do something useful— read some Shakespeare. He never played on the piano again for months, and for years never until he had ascertained that his father was out. "It was a mistake," he told me once, apropos of it. "If he had said that it disturbed him, but that I might do it later, I should have been delighted to stop. I always liked feeling that I was obliging people."

He disliked his father, and feared him. The tall, handsome gentleman, accustomed to be obeyed, in reality passionately fond of his children, dismayed him. He once wrote on a piece of paper the words, "I hate papa," and buried it in the garden.

For the rest, he was an ordinary, rather clever, secretive child, speaking very little of his feelings, and caring, as he has told me since, very little for anybody except his nurse. "I cared about her in a curious way. I enjoyed the sensation of crying over imaginary evils; and I should not like to say how often in bed at night I used to act over in my mind an imaginary death-bed scene of my nurse, and the pathetic remarks she was to make about Master Arthur, and the edifying bearing I was to show. This was calculated within a given time to produce tears, and then I was content."

He went to a private school, which he hated, and then to Winchester, which he grew to love. The interesting earnest little boy merged into the clumsy loose-jointed schoolboy, silent and languid. There are hardly any records of this time.

"My younger sister died," he told me, "when I was at school. I experienced about ten minutes of grief; my parents were overwhelmed with anguish, and I can remember that, like a quick, rather clever child, I soon came to comprehend the sort of remark that cheered them, and almost overdid it in my zeal. I am overwhelmed with shame," he said, "whenever I look at my mother's letters about that time when she speaks of the comfort I was to them. It was a *fraus pia*, but it was a most downright *fraus*."

I think I may relate one other curious incident among his public school experiences: it may seem very incredible, but I have his word for it that it is true.

"A sixth-form boy took a fancy to me, and let me sit in his room, and helped me in my work. The night before he left the school I was sitting there, and just before I went away, being rather overcome with regretful sentiments, he caught hold of me by the arm and said, among other things, 'And now that I am going away, and shall probably never see you again, I don't believe you care one bit.' I don't know how I came to do it," he said, "because I was never demonstrative; but I bent down and kissed him on the cheek, and then blushed up to my ears. He let me go at once; he was very much astonished, and I think not a little pleased; but it was certainly a curious incident."

During this time his intellectual development was proceeding slowly. "I went through three phases," he said. "I began by a curious love for pastoral and descriptive poetry. I read Thomson and Cowper, similes from 'Paradise Lost,' and other selections of my own; I read Tennyson, and revelled in the music of the lines and words. I intended to be a poet.

"Then I became omnivorous, and read everything, whether I understood it or not, especially biographies. I spent all my spare time in the school library; one only valuable thing have I derived from that—a capacity for taking in the sense of a page at a glance, and having a verbal memory of a skimmed book for an hour or two superior to any one that I ever met."

Then there came an ebb, and he read nothing, but loafed all day, and tried to talk. He had a notion he said, that he could argue Socratically; and he was always trying to introduce metaphors into his conversation. But his remarks in a much later letter to a friend on childish reading are so pertinent that I introduce them here.

"Never take a book away from a child unless it is positively vicious; that they should learn how to read a book and read it quickly is the great point; that they should get a habit of reading, and feel a void without it, is what should be cultivated. Never mind if it is trash now; their tastes will insensibly alter. I like a boy to cram himself with novels; a day will come when he is sick of them, and rejects them for the study of facts. What we want to give a child is 'bookmindedness,' as some one calls it. They will read a good deal that is bad, of course; but innocence is as slippery as a duck's back; a boy really fond of reading is generally pure-minded enough. When you see a robust, active, out-of-door boy deeply engrossed in a book, then you may suspect it if you like, and ask him what he has got; it will probably have an animal bearing."

Friendships more or less ardent, butterfly-hunting, school games, constant visits to the cathedral for service, to which he was always keenly devoted, uneventful holidays, filled up most of his school life. His letters at this date are very ordinary; his early precocity seemed, rather to the delight of his parents, to have vanished. He was not a prig, though rather exclusive; not ungenial, though retiring. "A dreadful boy," he writes of himself, "who is as mum as a mouse with his elders, and then makes his school friends roar with laughter in the passage: dumb at home, a chatterbox at school."

"I had no religion at that time," he writes, "with the exception of six months, when I got interested in it by forming a friendship with an attractive ritualistic curate; but my confirmation made no impression on me, and I think I had no moral feelings that I could distinguish. I had no inherent hatred of wrong, or love for right; but I was fastidious, and that kept me from being riotous, and undemonstrative, which made me pure."

CHAPTER II

Arthur went up to the University, Trinity College, Cambridge, in 1870; he did not distinguish himself there, or acquire more than he had done at Winchester: "The one thing I learnt at Winchester that has been useful to me since, was how to tie up old letters: my house-master taught me how to do that—it was about all he was fit for. The thing I learnt at Cambridge was to smoke: my cousin Fred taught me that, and he was hardly fit for that."

As it was at Cambridge that I first met him, I will give a short description of him as far as I can remember.

He was a tall, lounging fellow, rather clumsy in his movements, but with a kind of stateliness about him; he looked, and was, old for his years. He was a little short-sighted and wore glasses; without them his brow had that puzzled, slightly bothered look often seen in weak-sighted people. His face was not unattractive, though rather heavy; his hair was dark and curly—he let it grow somewhat long from indolence—and he had a drooping moustache. He was one of the men who, without the slightest idea of doing so, always managed to create rather an impression. As he lounged along the street with his hands in his pockets, generally alone, people used to turn and look at him. If he had taken a line of any kind he would have been known everywhere—but he did nothing.

The occasion on which I met him first was in the rooms of a common friend; there was a small gathering of men. He was sitting in a low chair, smoking intently. It was the one occupation he loved; he hardly said anything, though the conversation was very animated; silence was his latest phase; but as it was his first term, and he was not very well acquainted with the party, it appeared natural; not that being surrounded by dukes and bishops would have made the slightest difference to him if he had been disposed to talk, but he was not talkative, and held his tongue.

There had been some discussion about careers and their relative merits. One rather cynical man had broken in upon the ambitious projects that were being advanced with, "Well, we must remember that we are after all only average men."

"Yes," said Arthur, slowly, from the depths of his chair, "no doubt; only not quite so average."

The gentleman addressed, who was a senior man, stared for a moment at the freshman who had ventured to correct him, to whom he had not even been introduced; but Arthur was staring meditatively at the smoke rising from his pipe, and did not seem inclined to move or be moved, so he concluded not to continue the discussion.

The only other thing I heard him say that night was as follows. An ardent enthusiast on the subject of missions was present, who, speaking of an Indian mission lately started and apparently wholly ineffective, said, "But we must expect discouragement at first. The Church has always met with that."

"Yes," said Arthur; "but we must also remember, what people are very apt to forget, that ill success is not an absolute proof that God is on our side."

These two remarks, slight as they were, struck me; and, indeed, I have never quite forgotten that indefinable first impression of the man. There was a feeling about him of holding great things in reserve, an utter absence of self-consciousness, a sensation that he did not value the opinions of other people, that he did not regulate his conduct by them, which is very refreshing in these social days, when everybody's doings and sayings are ventilated and discussed so freely. He had none of the ordinary ambitions; he did not want a reputation, I thought, on ordinary grounds; he struck me as liking to observe and consider, not to do or say.

I am fond of guessing at character and forming impressions; and I very soon found out that these were not mistaken. My way that night lay with him as far as the gate of his college. We struck up a kind of acquaintanceship, though I felt conscious that he did not in the least care about doing so, that he probably would not give me another thought. It seems strange, reflecting on that evening, that I should now come to be his biographer.

However, I was interested in the type of character he displayed, and did not let the acquaintance drop. I invited him to my rooms. He would not come of his own accord at first, but by-and-by he got habituated to me, and not unfrequently strolled in.

He never let any one into the secret of his motives; he never confessed to any plans for the future, or to taking any interest in one line of life more than another. He was well off and did not spend much, except on his books, which were splendid. His rooms were untidy to the last degree, but liberally supplied with the most varied contrivances for obtaining a comfortable posture. Deep chairs and sofas, with devices for books and light, and for writing in any position. "When my mind is at work," he said to me once, "I don't like to be reminded of my body at all. I want to forget that I have one; and so I always say my prayers lying down."

He dressed badly, or rather carelessly, for he never gave the subject a moment's thought. If his friends told him that a suit was shabby, he appeared in a day or two in a new one, till that was similarly noticed; then it was discarded altogether. He always wore one suit till he had worn it out, never varying it. But he consulted fashion to a certain extent. "My object," he said, "is to escape notice, to look like every one else. I think of all despicable people, the people who try to attract attention by a marked style of dress, are perhaps the lowest."

His life at Cambridge was very monotonous, for he enjoyed monotony; he used to say that he liked to reflect on getting up in the morning, that his day was going to be filled by ordinary familiar things. He got up rather late, read his subjects for an hour or two, strolled about to see one or two friends, lunched with them or at home, strolled in the afternoon, often dropping in to King's for the anthem, went back to his rooms for tea, the one time at which he liked to see his friends, read or talked till hall, and finally settled down to his books again at ten, reading till one or two in the morning.

He read very desultorily and widely. Thus he would read books on Arctic voyages for ten days and talk of nothing else, then read novels till he sickened for facts and fact till he sickened for fiction; biographies, elementary science, poetry, general philosophy, particularly delighting in any ideal theories of life and discipline in state or association, but with a unique devotion to "Hamlet" and "As You Like It," the "Pilgrim's Progress," and Emerson's "Representative Men." He rarely read the Bible, he told me, and then only in great masses at a sitting; and the one thing that he disliked with an utter hatred was theology of a settled and orthodox type, though next to the four books I have mentioned, "The Christian Year" and "Ecce Homo" were his constant companions.

He did not care for history; he used to lament it. "I have but a languid interest in facts, qua facts," he said; "and I try to arrive at history through biography. I like to disentangle the separate strands, one at a time; the fabric is too complex for me."

He had the greatest delight in topography. "That is why," he used to say, "I delight in a flat country. The idea of *space* is what I want. I like to see miles at a glance. I like to see clouds league-long rolling up in great masses from the horizon—cloud perspective. I rejoice in seeing the fields, hedgerow after hedgerow, farm after farm, push into the blue distance. It makes me feel the unity and the diversity of life; a city bewilders and confuses me, but a great tract of placid country gives me a broad glow of satisfaction."

He went for a walking tour in the fens, and returned enchanted. "By Ely," he said, "the line crosses a gigantic fen—Whittlesea mere in old days—and on a clear day you can see at least fifteen miles either way. As we crossed it a great skein of starlings rose out of a little holt, and streamed north; the herons or quiet cattle stood along the huge dykes. You could see the scattered figures of old labourers in the fields, and then for miles and miles the squat towers, at which you were making, staring over the flat, giving you a thrill every time you sighted them, and right away west the low hills that must have been the sandy downs that blocked the restless plunging sea; they must have looked for centuries over rollers and salt marsh and lagoon, felt the tread of strange herds and beasts about them till they have become the quiet slopes of a sunny park or the simple appendages of a remote hill farm."

But his greatest delight was in music. He knew a smattering of it scientifically, enough to follow up subjects and to a certain extent to recognize chords. There occurs in one of his letters to me the following passage, which I venture to quote. He is speaking of the delight of pure sound as apart from melody:

"I remember once," he writes, "being with a great organist in a cathedral organ-loft, sitting upon the bench at his side. He was playing a Mass of Schubert's, and close to the end, at the last chord but two—he was dying to a very soft close, sliding in handles all over the banks of stops—he nodded with his head to the rows of pedal stops with their red labels, as though to indicate where danger lay. 'Put your hand on the thirty-two foot,' he said. There it was '*Double open wood 32 ft.*' And just as his fingers slid on to the last chord, 'Now,' he said.

"Ah! that was it; the great wooden pipe close to my ear began to blow and quiver; and hark! not sound, but sensation—the great rapturous stir of the air; a drowsy thunder in the roof of nave and choir; the grim saints stirred and rattled ill their leaded casements, while the melodious roar died away as softly as it had begun, sinking to silence with many a murmurous pulsation, many a throb of sighing sound."

Organ-playing, organ music, was the one subject on which I have heard him wax enthusiastic. His talk and his letters always become rhetorical when he deals with music; his musical metaphors are always carefully worked out; he compares a man of settled purpose, in whose life the "motive was very apparent," to "the great lazy horns, that you can always hear in the orchestra pouring out their notes hollow and sweet, however loud the violins shiver or the trumpets cry." He often went up to London to hear music. The St. James's Hall Concerts were his especial delight. I find later a description of the effect produced on him by Wagner.

"I have just come back from the Albert Hall, from hearing the 'Meistersänger,' Wagner himself conducting. I may safely say I think that I never experienced such absolute artistic rapture before as at certain parts of this; for instance, in the overture, at one place where the strings suddenly cease and there comes a peculiar chromatic waft of wind instruments, like a ghostly voice rushing across. I have never felt anything like it; it swept one right away, and gave one a sense of deep ineffable satisfaction. I shall always feel *for the future* that there is an existent region, *into which I have now actually penetrated*, in which that entire satisfaction is possible, a fact which I have always hitherto doubted. It is like an initiation.

"But I can not bear the 'Tannhäuser;' it seems to paint with a fatal fascination the beauty of wickedness, the rightness, so to speak, of sensuality. I feel after it as if I had been yielding to a luscious temptation; unnerved, not inspired."

In another letter he writes, "Music is the most hopeful of the arts; she does not hint only, like other expressions of beauty—she takes you straight into a world of peace, a world where law and beauty are the same, and where an ordered discord, that is discord working by definite laws, is the origin of the keenest pleasure."

I remember, during the one London season which he subsequently went through, his settling himself at a Richter concert next me with an air of delight upon his face. "Now," he said, "let us try and remember for an hour or two that we have souls."

CHAPTER III

I must here record one curious circumstance which I have never explained even to my own satisfaction.

He had been at Cambridge about two years, when, in the common consent of all his friends, his habits and behaviour seemed to undergo a complete and radical change.

I have never discovered what the incident was that occasioned this change; all I know is that suddenly, for several weeks, his geniality of manner and speech, his hilarity, his cheerfulness, entirely disappeared; a curious look of haunting sadness, not defined, but vague, came over his face; and though he gradually returned to his old ways, yet I am conscious myself, and others would support me in this, that he was never quite the same again; he was no longer young.

The only two traces that I can discover in his journals, or letters, or elsewhere, of the facts are these.

He always in later diaries vaguely alludes to a certain event which changed his view of things in general; "ever since," "since that November," "for now nearly five years I have felt." These and similar phrases constantly occur in his diary. I will speak in a moment of what nature I should conjecture it to have been.

A packet of letters in his desk were marked "to be burnt unopened;" but at the same time carefully docketed with dates: these dates were all immediately after that time, extending over ten days.

The exact day was November 8, 1872. It is engraved in a small silver locket that hung on his watch-chain, where he was accustomed to have important days in his life marked, such as the day he adopted his boy, his mother's death. It is preceded by the Greek letters ΒΠ, which from a certain entry in his diary I conceive to be $\beta\acute{\alpha}\pi\tau\iota\sigma\mu\alpha$ $\pi\upsilon\varrho\grave{o}\varsigma$, "the baptism of fire."

Lastly, in a diary for that year, kept with fair regularity up till November 8, there here intervenes a long blank, the only entry being November 9: "Salvum me fac, Dne."

I took the trouble, incidentally, to hunt up the files of a Cambridge journal of that date, to see if I could link it on to any event, and I found there recorded, in the course of that week, what I at first imagined to be the explanation of the incidents, and own I was a good deal surprised.

I found recorded some Revivalist Mission Services, which were then held in Cambridge with great success. I at once concluded that he underwent some remarkable spiritual experience, some religious fright, some so-called conversion, the effects of which only gradually disappeared. The contagion of a Revivalist meeting is a very mysterious thing. Like a man going to a mesmerist, an individual may go, announcing his firm intention not to be influenced in the smallest degree by anything said or done. Nay more, he may think himself, and have the reputation of being, a strong, unyielding character, and yet these are the very men who are often most hopelessly mesmerized, the very men whom the Revival most absolutely—for the occasion—enslaves. And thus, knowing that one could form no *prima facie* judgments on the probabilities in such a matter, I came to the conclusion that he had fallen, in some degree, under the influence of these meetings.

But in revising this book, and carefully recalling my own and studying others' impressions, I came to the conclusion that it was impossible that this should be the case.

1. In the first place, he was more free than any man I ever saw from the influence of contagious emotions; he dissembled his own emotions, and contemned the public display of them in other people.

2. He had, I remember, a strange repugnance, even abhorrence, to public meetings in the later days at Cambridge. I can now recall that he would accompany people to the door, but never be induced to enter. A passage which I will quote from one of his letters illustrates this.

"The presence of a large number of people has a strange, repulsive physical effect on me. I feel crushed and overwhelmed, not stimulated and vivified, as is so often described. I can't listen to a concert comfortably if there is a great throng, unless the music is so good as to wrap one altogether away. There is undoubtedly a force abroad among large masses of people, the force which forms the basis of the principle of public prayer, and I am conscious of it too, only it distresses me; moreover, the worst and most afflicting nightmare I have is the sensation of standing sightless and motionless, but with all the other senses alert and apprehensive, in the presence of a vast and hostile crowd."

3. He never showed the least sign of being influenced in the direction of spiritual or even religious life by this crisis. He certainly spoke very little at all for some time to any one on any subject; he was distrait and absent-minded in society—for the alteration was much observed from its suddenness—but when he gradually began to converse as usual, he did not, as is so often the case in similar circumstances, do what is called "bearing witness to the truth." His attitude toward all enthusiastic forms of religion had been one, in old days, of good-natured, even amused tolerance. He was now not so good-natured in his criticisms, and less sparing of them, though his religious-mindedness, his seriousness, was undoubtedly increased by the experience, whatever it was.

On the whole, then, I should say that the coincidence of the revival is merely fortuitous. It remains to seek what the cause was.

We must look for it, in a character so dignified as Arthur's, in some worthy cause, some emotional failure, some moral wound. I believe the following to be the clew; I can not develop it without treading some rather delicate ground.

He had formed, in his last year at school, a very devoted friendship with a younger boy; such friendships like the εἰσπνήλας and the ἀΐτάς of Sparta, when they are truly chivalrous and absolutely pure, are above all other loves, noble, refining, true; passion at white heat without taint, confidence of so intimate a kind as can not even exist between husband and wife, trust such as can not be shadowed, are its characteristics. I speak from my own experience, and others will, I know, at heart confirm me, when I say that these things are infinitely rewarding, unutterably dear.

Arthur left Winchester. A correspondence ensued between the two friends. I have three letters of Arthur's, so passionate in expression, that for fear of even causing uneasiness, not to speak of suspicion, I will not quote them. I have seen, though I have destroyed, at request, the letters of the other.

This friend, a weak, but singularly attractive boy, got into a bad set at Winchester, and came to grief in more than one way; he came to Cambridge in three years, and fell in with a thoroughly bad set there. Arthur seems not to have suspected it at first, and to have delighted in his friend's society; but such things as habits betray themselves, and my belief is that disclosures were made on November 8, which revealed to Arthur the state of the case. What passed I can not say. I can hardly picture to myself the agony, disgust, and rage (his words and feelings about sensuality of any kind were strangely keen and bitter), loyalty fighting with the sense of repulsion, pity struggling with honour, which must have convulsed him when he discovered that his friend was not only yielding, but deliberately impure.

The other's was an unworthy and brutal nature, utterly corrupted at bottom. He used to speak jestingly of the occurrence. "Oh yes!" I have heard him say; "we were great friends once, but he cuts me now; he had to give me up, you see, because he didn't approve of me. Justice, mercy, and truth, and all the rest of it."

It was certainly true; their friendship ended. I find it hard to realize that Arthur would voluntarily have abandoned him; and yet I find passages in his letters, and occasional entries in his diaries, which seem to point to some great stress put upon him, some enormous burden indicated, which he had not strength to attempt and adopt. "May God forgive me for my unutterable selfishness; it is irreparable now," is one of the latest entries on that day in his diary. I conceive, perhaps, that his outraged ideal was too strong for his power of forgiveness. He was very fastidious, always.

How deep the blow cut will be shown by these following extracts:

"I once had my faith in human nature rudely wrecked, and it has never attempted a long voyage again. I hug the coast and look regretfully out to sea; perhaps the day may come when I may strike into it ... believe in it always if you can; I do not say it is vanity ... the shock blinded me; I can not see if I would."

And again—

"Moral wounds never heal; they may be torn open by a chance word, by a fragment of print, by a sentence from a letter; and there we have to sit with pale face and shuddering heart, to bleed in silence and dissemble it. Then, too, there is that constant dismal feeling which the Greeks called ὕπουλος: the horrible conviction, the grim memory lurking deep down, perhaps almost out of sight, thrust away by circumstance and action, but always ready to rise noiselessly up and draw you to itself."

"'A good life, and therefore a happy one,' says my old aunt, writing to me this morning; it is marvellous and yet sustaining what one can pass through, and yet those about you—those who suppose that they have the key, if any, to your heart—be absolutely ignorant of it. 'He looks a little tired and worn: he has been sitting up late;' 'all young men are melancholy: leave him alone and he will be better in a year or two,' was all that was said when I was actually meditating suicide—when I believe I was on the brink of insanity."

All these extracts are from letters to myself at different periods. Taking them together, and thus arranged, my case seems irresistible; still I must concede that it is all theory—all inference: I do not wholly know the facts, and never shall.

CHAPTER IV

I found the first hint that occurs to indicate the lines of his later life, in a letter to his father, written in his last week at Cambridge. In the Classical Tripos Arthur contrived to secure a second; in the translations, notably Greek, we heard he did as well as anybody; but history and other detailed subjects dragged him down: it was an extraordinarily unequal performance.

His father, being ambitious for his sons, and knowing to a certain extent Arthur's ability, was altogether a good deal disappointed. He had accepted Arthur's failure to get a scholarship or exhibition, not with equanimity, but with a resolute silence, knowing that strict scholarship was not his son's strong point, but still hoping that he would at least do well enough in his Tripos to give him a possibility of a Fellowship.

Arthur would himself have been happier with a Fellowship than with any other position, but the possibility did not stimulate him to work with that aim in view. He wrote: "Existence generally is so extremely problematical, that I can not consent to throw away three birds in the hand for one which I do not believe to be in the bush—my present life for a doubtful future provision. I think I am ambitious after the event. Every normal human being ought to be capable either of strong expectation or strong disappointment, according as the character lives most in the future or in the past. Those capable of both generally succeed and are unhappy men; but an entire want of ambition argues a low vitality. If a man tells me loftily he has no ambition, I tell him I am very sorry for him, and say that it is almost as common an experience as having no principles, and often accompanying it, only that people are generally ashamed to confess the latter."

On his appearing in the second class, his father wrote him rather an indignant letter, saying that he had suspected all along that he was misusing his time and wasting his opportunities, but that he had refrained from saying so because he had trusted him; that his one prayer for his children was that they might not turn out useless, dilettante, or frivolous, selfish men. "I had hoped that whatever they engaged in my sons would say, 'If this is worth doing, it is worth doing well.' I did not want them to say, 'I mean to work in order to be first in this or that, to beat other people, to court success'—I do not suspect you of that—but to say, 'I mean to do my best, and if I am rewarded with honours to accept them gratefully, as a sign that my endeavours have been blest.' I fear that in your case you have done what pleased yourself—sucked the honey of the work, or tried to; that always ends in bitterness. You were capable of taking the higher ground; it seems to me that you have taken neither—and indecision in such matters is the one thing that does not succeed either in this world or the next; the one thing which the children of this world unanimously agree with the children of light in despising and censuring.

"P.S.—You used to speak of possibly taking orders; set to work seriously on that if you haven't changed your mind; for that is what I have always hoped and prayed for you. Let me see that you are capable of executing as well as planning a high resolve finely."

Arthur's behaviour on receiving this letter was very characteristic. He did not answer it.

It was a habit he had which got him into considerable odium with people. Whenever a letter entailed making up his mind—an invitation which had two sides to it—a decision—a request for advice or immediate action—these rarely extorted an answer from him. "It did not seem to me to be very important," he used to say. Neither would he be dictated to. A friend who had asked him to form one of a football eleven, receiving no reply, inclosed two post-cards addressed to himself, on one of which was written "Yes," and on the other "No." Arthur posted them both.

But a casual letter, implying friendliness, a statement of mental or moral difficulties, criticisms on an interesting book, requests involving principles, drew out immediate, full, and interesting replies, of apparently almost unnecessary urgency and affection. A boy who wrote to him from school about a long and difficult moral case, infinitely complicated by side issues and unsatisfactory action, got back the following day an exhaustive, imperative, and yet pleading reply, indicating the proper action to take. It is far too private to quote; but for pathos and lucidity and persuasiveness it is a wonderful document.

But this letter of his father's he did not answer for ten days, till the last day but one before his leaving Cambridge, neither did he mention the subject. I do not think he gave it a thought, except as one might consider an unpleasant matter of detail which required to be finished sometime.

On that day there arrived another note from his father, recapitulating what he had said, and saying that he supposed from his silence that he had not received the former letter.

To this Arthur returned the following letter:

"Trinity College, Cambridge, Thursday evening (early in 1874).

"My Dear Father:

"I don't wish you to be under any misapprehension about your former letter. I did receive it and have been carefully considering the subject; it seemed to me that I could better say what I wished in a personal interview, and I therefore refrained from writing till I came home; but you seem to wish me to make an immediate statement, which I will briefly do.

"You must not think that what I am going to say is in the least disrespectful. I assure you that I gave your letter, as coming from you, a consideration that I should not have thought of extending for a moment to any other man except one or two friends for whose opinion I have the highest respect; but it is a subject upon which, though I can not exactly say that my mind is made up, yet I see so distinctly which way my disposition lies and in what direction my opinions are capable of undergoing change, that I may say I have very little doubt—it is, in short, almost a fixed conviction.

"The moment when any one finds himself in radical opposition to the traditions in which he was brought up is very painful—I can assure you of that—to himself, as I fear it is painful to those from whom he dissents; and nothing but a desire for absolute sincerity would induce me to enter upon it. But knowing and trusting you as I do, with a firm and filial confidence in your loving thoughts and candid open-mindedness, I venture to say exactly what I think, believing that it would be a far more essential disrespect to endeavour to blink those opinions.

"Shortly, I do *not* believe that practical usefulness of a direct kind is the end of life. I do *not* believe that success is either a test of greatness nor, as you suggest, an adequate aim for it, though you will perhaps excuse me if I say that the reasons you give seem to me to be only the material view skillfully veiled.

"I do not feel in my own mind assured that the highest call in my case is to engage in a practical life. In fact, I feel fairly well assured that it is not. I do not know that I intend deliberately to shirk the responsibilities of moral action which fall in every feeling man's way. I rather mean that I shall face them from the ordinary standpoint, and not thrust myself into any position where helping my fellow-creatures is merely an official act. I think shortly that by the plan I have vague thoughts of pursuing I may gain an influence among minds which will certainly be, if I win it, of a very high kind. I dare not risk the possibilities by flying at lower game.

"Besides, I do not feel nearly enough assured of my ground to say that active work, as you describe it, is either advisable or necessary. I want to examine and consider, to turn life and thought inside out, to see if I can piece together in the least the enormous problem of which God has flung us the fragments. I do not despair of arriving at some inkling of that truth. I shall try, if I gain it, to communicate that glimmering to others, if that is God's will for me; if not, perhaps I shall be a little wiser or a little happier, at least a little more capable of receiving my illumination, when the time for that comes.

"I don't feel as if I understood at all clearly what is God's purpose for individuals. I can't take public opinion for granted. I will not let it overwhelm me. I want to stand aside and think; and my own prayer for my own children, if I had them, would rather be that they might be saved from being effective, when I see all the evils which success and mere effectiveness bring.

"What I had thought of doing was of going abroad for a year or two; but in that matter I am entirely in your hands, because I am dependent on you. I consider travel not a luxury, but a necessity. If you will make me an allowance for that purpose I shall very gladly accept it. If not, I shall endeavour to get some post where I may make enough money to take me where I wish to go. I shall throw myself upon the power 'who providently caters for the sparrows' after that.

"I propose to come home on Friday for a week or two. This letter contains only a draft of what I should have preferred to say there in words.

"I am your affectionate son,
"Arthur Hamilton."

His father curtly acknowledged this letter, but nothing more; and left the discussion of the subject to be a personal one. They came to the following compromise.

Arthur was to engage for one year in some active profession, business, the law, medicine, schoolmastering, taking pupils; at the end of that time he was to make his choice; if he decided not to take up any profession, his father promised to allow him £350 a year as long as he lived, and to secure him the same sum after his own death. This occupation was to extend from August till the August following. He was allowed three days for his decision.

He at once decided on schoolmastering, and without much difficulty secured a post at an upper-class private school, being a substantial suburban house, in fine timbered grounds, the boys being all destined for public schools.

He wrote me several letters from that place, but during that time our correspondence waned, as we were both very busy. He was interested in his work, and very popular with the boys.

"My experience of life generally gives me a strong impulse in favour of Determinism; that is to say, the system which considers the histories of nations, the lives of individuals, their very deeds and words, to be all part of a vast unalterable design: and whose dealing with the past, with each event, indeed, as it occurs, is thus nothing but interpretation, an earnest endeavour to exclude regret or disappointment, and to see how best to link each fact in our past on with what we know of ourselves, to see its bearing on our individual case. Of course this will operate with our view of the future too, but only in a general way, to minimize ambition and anxiety. It produces, in fact, exactly the same effect as a perfect 'faith;' indeed, it is hard to distinguish the two, except that faith is the instinctive practice of the theory of Determinism.

"Now, the more I work at education, the more I am driven into Determinism; it seems that we can hardly regulate tendency, in fact as if the schoolmaster's only duty was to register change. A boy comes to a place like this, μνημονὶκος and φιλομάθης, and εὐφύης, as Ascham calls it, in other respects; he is not exposed, let us say, to any of the temptations which extraordinary charms of face or manner seem always to entail upon their possessors, and he leaves it just the same, except that the natural propensities are naturally developed; whereas a boy with precisely the same educational and social advantages but without a predisposition to profit by them leaves school hardly altered in person or mind. It is true that circumstances alter character—that can not be disputed; but circumstances are precisely what we can not touch. A boy, εὐφύης as I have described, brought up as a street-arab, would only so far profit by it as to be slightly less vicious and disgusting than his companions. But education, which we speak of as a panacea for all ills, only deals with what it finds, and does not, as we ought to claim, rub down bad points and accentuate good, and it is this, that perhaps more than anything else has made me a Determinist, that the very capacity for change and improvement is so native to some characters, and so utterly lacking to others. A man can in real truth do nothing of himself, though there are all possible varieties—from the man who can see his deficiencies and make them up, through the man who sees his weak points and can not strengthen them, to the spiritually blind who can not even see them. I may of course belong to the latter class myself—it is the one thing about which no one can decide for himself—but an inherent contempt for certain parts of my character seems to hint to me that it is not so."

It will be seen from the last two letters that his ethical position was settling itself.

I therefore think, before I go any further, it will be as well to give a short account of his religious opinions at this time, as they were very much bound up with his life. He told me not unfrequently that religion had been nothing whatever to him at school, and he came up to the University impressionable, ardent, like a clean paper ready for any writing.

It is well known that at the Universities there is a good deal of proselytizing; that it is customary for men of marked religious views and high position to have a large *clientèle* of younger men whom they influence and mould; schools of the prophets.

Arthur was not drawn into any one of these completely, though I fancy that he was to a certain extent influenced by the teaching of one of these men. The living original of these words will pardon me if I here insert the words of my friend relating to him; many Cambridge men have been and are everlastingly grateful for his simple noble influence and example.

"Why are there certain people in this world, who whenever they enter a room have a strange power of galvanizing everybody there into connection with themselves? what mysterious currents do they set in motion to and from them, so that those who do not talk to them or at them, begin to talk with reference to them, hedged about as they are with an atmosphere of desire and command?

"There is one of these at Cambridge now, a man for whom I not only have the profoundest respect, but whose personal presence exercises on me just the fascination I describe; and influential as he is, it is influence more utterly unconscious of its own power than any I have seen—a rare quality. He finds all societies into which he enters, stung by his words and looks, serious, sweet, interested in, if not torn by moral and social problems of the deepest import; yet he always fancies that it is they, not he, that are thus potent. He is not aware that it is he who is saintly; he thinks it is they that are good; and all this, not for want of telling him, for he must be weary of genuine praise and thanks."

To write thus of any one must imply a deep attraction. I do not think, however, that the admiration ever extended itself to imitation in matters theoretical or religious. Arthur was not one of those indiscriminate admirers, blinded by a single radiant quality to accept the whole body as full of light.

Very slowly his convictions crystallized; he had a period of very earnest thought—during the time of which I have just been speaking—in which he shunned the subject in conversation; but I have reason to believe from the books he read, and from two or three letters to his friend, the curate of whom I have been speaking, that he was thinking deeply upon revealed religion.

It must, however, be remembered that he never went through that period of agonized uprooting of venerated and cherished sentiment that many whose faith has been very keen and integral in their lives pass through, the dark valley of doubt. His religion had not intwined itself into his life; it was not shrined among his sacred memories or laid away in secret storehouses of thought.

"I have never felt the agony of a dying faith," he wrote to a friend who was sorely troubled, "so you will forgive me if I do not seem to sympathize very delicately with you, or if I seem not to understand the darkness you are in. But I have been in deep waters myself, though of another kind. I have seen an old ideal foully shattered in a moment, and a hope that I had held and that had consecrated my life for many years, not only crushed in an instant—that would have been bad enough—but its place filled by an image of despair ... so you will see that I *can* feel for you, as I *do*.

"Leading to the light is a sad, terribly sad, and wearying process; I have not won it yet, but I have seen glimpses which have dispelled a gloom which I thought was hopeless. My dear friend, I *know* that God will bring you out into a place of liberty, as He has brought me; in the day when you come and tell me that He has done so, the smile that will be on your face will be no sort of symbol, I know, of the unutterable content within. *Expertus novi,* you have my thoughts and hopes."

The letters I shall now quote are taken out of a considerable period, and give a fair picture of what he believed. Tolerance was his great characteristic.

Below all principles of his own was a deep resolve not to interfere in any way with the principles of others, however erroneous he deemed them.

With his definition of sincerity that comes out in the following extracts I have myself often found fault in conversation and by letter, but I never produced any change. I thought, and still think, that it is sophistical in tone, and tampers with one of the most sacred of our instincts. It never in his case, I think, made any difference to his presentment of the truth, but it is a principle that I should not dare to advocate; however, it was so integral a part of his faith that in this delineation, which shall be as accurate as I can make it, I dare not omit it.

His convictions were then a steady accumulation, not the shreds of one system worked into the fabric by the overmastering new impulse communicated by another, as is so often the case. He writes:

"The strong man's house entered by the stronger, and his goods despoiled, is a parable more frequently true of the conversion of a 'believer' into a sceptic than *vice versa*. The habit of firm adherence to principle, the capacity for trust, the adaptation of intellectual resources to uphold a theory—all these go to swell the new emotion; no man is so effective a sceptic as the man who has been a fervent believer.

"But in the rare cases of the conversion of an intellectual man from scepticism into belief (like Augustine and a very few others) the spirit suffers by the change. A great deal of cultivation, of logical readiness, of eloquence, seem to be essentially secular, to belong essentially to the old life, and to need imperatively putting away together with the garment spotted by the flesh. Augustine suffered less perhaps than others; but some diminution of force seems an inevitable result.

"I never had a great change of that kind to make. I had a moral awakening, which was rude but effective, never a conversion; I had not to strike my old colours."

Thus, though he was a strong Determinist, his capacity for idealism, and a natural enthusiasm, saved him from the paralysis which in some cases results from such speculations.

"I look upon all philosophical theories as explanations of an ontological problem, not as a basis of action. The appearance of free-will in adopting or discontinuing a course of action is a deception, but it is a complete deception—so complete as not to affect in the slightest my interest in what is going to happen, nor my unconscious posing as a factor in that result. Though I am only a cogwheel in a vast machine, yet I am conscious of my cogs, interested in my motions and the motions of the whole machine, though ignorant of who is turning, why he began, and whether he will stop, and why.

"If I saw the slightest loophole at which free-will might creep in, I would rush to it, but I do not; if man was created with a free will, he was also created with predispositions which made the acting of that will a matter of mathematical certainty.

"But the idea that it diminishes my interest in life or its issues is preposterous; I am inclined to credit God with larger ideas than my own, and His why and wherefore, and the part I bear in it, is extraordinarily fascinating to me because it is so hidden; and the least indication of law that I can seize upon—such as this law of necessity—is an entrancing glimpse into reality. It may not be quite so delightful as some other theories, but it is true, and real, and therefore has an actual working in you and me and every one else, which can not fail to attach a certain interest to it which other systems lack."

He gives a very graphic illustration of the phenomena of free-will. He says—

"It seems to me closely to resemble a very ordinary phenomenon: the principle that things as they are farther off appear to us to be smaller. Logical reflection assures us that they are not so, but the effect upon our senses is completely illusive; and, what is more, we act as though they were smaller; we act as if what they gained in distance they lost in size; we aim at a target which is many feet high and broad as if it was but a few inches; we say the sun is about as big as a soup-plate, and having once made these allowances the knowledge does not affect our conduct of life at all.

"Just so with free-will; we know by our reason that the thing is impossible; we act as though it were a prevailing possibility."

His position with regard to Christianity was shortly as follows; it is settled by an extract from his diary:

"I have often puzzled over this: Why in the Gospels did Christ say nothing about the whole fabric of nature which in His capacity as Creator ('through whom He made all things') He must have had the moulding of? All His teaching was personal and individual, dealing with man alone, an infinitesimal part of His creation ... for compare the shred, the span of being which man's existence represents with the countless æons of animal and vegetable life which have preceded, and surround, and will in all probability succeed it—and not a word of all this from the Being who gave and supported their life, calling it out of the abyss for inscrutable and useless ends—to minister, as the theologians tell us, to the wants and animal cravings of pitiful mankind.

"Why is it that He there takes no cognizance of the whole frame of things of which I am a part, but only deals with human feelings and emotions as if they were the end of all these gigantic works—the Milky Way, the blazing sun, the teeming earth—only to raise thoughts of reverence in the heart of this pitiful being, and failing too, so hopelessly, so constantly to do so?...

"'I will accept Christ,' said Herbert, 'as my superior, yes! as my master, yes! but not as my God.'" One sees, I think, where the difficulty lies; it must be felt by any man whose idea of God is very high, whose belief in humanity very low.

And again—

"I believe in a revelation which is coming, which may be among us now, though we do not suspect it, in the words and deeds of some simple-minded heroic man.

"No one who preceded the Christian revelation could possibly, from the fabric of the world as it then was, have anticipated the form it was about to take. This revelation, too, will be as unexpected as it will be new—it will come in the night as a thief; the '*quo modo*' I can not even attempt to guess, except that it will take the form of some vast simplification of the myriad and complicated issues of human life."

But such entries as these were left to his diaries and most private correspondence; he never attempted a crusade against ordinary forms of belief, mistaken though he deemed them, often putting a strong constraint upon himself in conversation. If he was pressed to give an account of his religious principles he used smilingly to say that he belonged to the great Johnsonian sect, who practised the religion of all sensible men, and who kept what it was to themselves.

There were two views of life with which he had no patience only—the men who preached the open confession of agnosticism, "if you have anything to tell us for goodness sake let us have it, but if you have not, hold your tongue; you are like a clock that has gone wrong, but insists on chiming to show everybody that it hasn't the least idea of the time;" and secondly, the men who "took no interest" in the problems of religion and morals; for a deliberate avoidance of them he had some respect, but for a professional moralist who took everything for granted, and for feeble materialists who did not "trouble their head" about such things, he had a profound contempt.

The following remarks that he gave vent to on the subject of orthodox Christianity and an Established Church are very striking, and after what has preceded might appear paradoxical and ridiculous. But they are in reality absolutely consistent.

"When people tell me," he said, "as you have been doing, that the old methods are *passés*, and compare the crude new ideas with them for effectiveness, as working theories, I snap my fingers mentally in their face.

"These new ideas may, and doubtless do, contain all the good of the world's future, all the seed of progress in them—but as working ideas! A system that has been mellowed and coloured, that has insinuated itself year by year into all the irregularities and whimsical, capricious, unexpected chinks and crannies of human nature, accommodating itself gradually to all, to be torn out and have the bleeding sensitive gap filled with a hard angular heavy object thrust straight in from an intellectual workshop—the idea is absolutely preposterous!"

A friend wrote to him once in great perplexity about the following problem: as to whether, taking as he did, a purely agnostic view of life, he should continue to receive the Communion with his parents when at home; as to whether it was not a base concession to his own weakness; as to whether he should not stand by his principles.

"If you have any principles to stand by," he wrote, "by all means stand by them; but if all you mean is throwing cold water on other people's principles, my advice is to make no move. Dissembling your own uneasiness in the matter and quieting their anxious scruples is one of those matters which seem so simple that heroism appears to have no part in it. It would be so much nobler (we are tempted to think) to stand up and protest and denunciate; to throw gloom and dissension into a happy home and wreck (if you are the affectionate son I believe you to be) your own happiness, not to speak of usefulness. It would be more arduous, I admit; not therefore nobler. Your duty is most plain; you have no right to cause acute distress to several people, because you can not take exactly such an exalted view as they do, of an institution which, from the lowest point of view, is the dying request of a great and loving soul, to all who can feel his beauty or listen to his call, a beautiful pledge of family and national unity, and a touching symbol of all good things."

To another friend, who wrote to him to say that his principles, though still religious, and faithful in general idea to the Christian creed, were in so many points different from the principles taught and demanded by the Church of England, that he felt he ought to take some definite step to show his state of mind, he wrote as follows:

"The being born into an institution is a thing which must not be lightly considered: it imposes certain duties upon you—the quiet examination of its tenets, for example—and unless you are convinced of its utter inutility, not to say immorality, it is your duty to bear such a part in relation to it as shall not mar its usefulness; and you may no more throw it away through caprice or indifferentism than you may throw away your own life, simply because you did not agree to be in the world, and it is through no will of your own that you are there. Similarly, you can not justify murder because you were not present to give an assent to the framing of the laws which condemn it and provide for its restraint.

"In fact, by taking such a step you are incurring a very heavy responsibility, and it is at any rate worth while to give it the closest consideration.

"And therefore I should suggest that the philosopher who wishes in any way to affect humanity for the better, should not begin his crusade by storming one of its chief defences because its title to that position is not quite so secure as the governor alleges; but rather accept his religion together with his life, his circumstances, his disposition, as a condition under which he is born: tacitly συνειδὼς ἑαύτῳ that it may not be absolute truth, from which no appeal is possible, but yet fight his best under its colours, though they may not be quite red enough to suit his own fancy.

"For what is there ignoble in this concealment? Is it not rather ignoble to demolish a hope on which others build because it does not appear to us to be quite satisfactory, though we have nothing to offer in its stead? It is like plucking down a savage's wattled cabin. 'First-rate stone houses, if you please, or none at all,'—and, on being questioned as to where the materials are to come from, point for answer to the eternal hills.

"These are general considerations; but you, in particular, my dear C——, ought to be very cautious, considering who you are." His father was a high dignitary of the church. "A secession like yours will carry far more weight than it ought to from your own and your father's position. People will say, Mr. C—— ought to know; he has had opportunities of judging from the inside which other people have not—whereas you have really less opportunity because your horizon is far more limited because you have only seen it from the inside. You are rather in the position of the valet. No gossip and gabble of yours about braces and sock-suspenders will make your hero less a hero: you will only establish your title to be considered an unperceptive and low-minded creature among the only people whose opinion is worth having."

He was always very decided on what he called "mock sincerity," the people whom he described as "professional crystals," who always "speak their mind about a thing." "The art of life," he said, "consists in knowing exactly what to keep out of sight at any given moment, and what to produce; when to play hearts and diamonds, ugly clubs or flat spades; and you must remember that every suit is trumps in turn."

The following passage from a letter about a leading politician will illustrate this:

"I have always admired him intensely," he writes, as an instance of a public man who has succeeded by sheer adherence to principles.

"You can't ensure success; three parts is luck, the genius of time and place. The only thing you can do seems to me to work hard, and always take the highest line about things. The highest line, that is to say, not the line you may *feel* to be highest, but the line that you *recognize* to be so. Not what your fluctuating emotions may commend, but that which the best moral tact seems to pronounce best. You can't always expect to feel enthusiasm for the best, so be true not to your sensations, but your deliberate ideals—that is the highest sincerity; all the higher because it is so often called hypocrisy."

But his Determinist, almost Calvinistic, views were mellowed and tempered by a serene and deep belief in a providence moving to good, and ordering life down to the smallest details with special reference to each man's case; in fact, as he said, the two were so closely connected that they were like the convex and concave sides of a lens.

He wrote to me, "I often feel, when straining after happiness, just like the child who, anxious to get home, pushes against the side of the railway carriage which is carrying him so smoothly and serenely to the haven where he would be, while all he effects is a temporary disarrangement of particles.

"Life shows me more and more every day that there is something watching us and working with us, so that now and then in unexpected moments when I have felt particularly independent for some time back, I come upon a little fact or incident that reveals to me that I am like a mouse in the grasp of a cat, allowed sometimes to run a few inches alone—or more truly like a baby walking along, very proud of its performance, with a couple of anxious, loving arms poised to catch it. The extraordinary apportionment not only in balance but in *kind* of punishment to sin—long-continued, secret, base desires, punished by long-hidden suffering—the sharp stress of temptation yielded to, requited by the sharp pang—the glorious feeling which I have once or twice felt—the sin once sinned and the punishment once over, as one is assured supremely sometimes that it is without doubt—of trustful freedom, and fresh fitness for battling one's self and helping others to battle—a mood that is soon broken, but is an earnest while it lasts of infinite satisfaction. The extraordinary delicacy with which the screw of pain and mental suffering is adjusted, just lifted when we can bear no more (not when *we* think we can bear no more, but when God knows it) and resolutely applied again when we have gained strength which we propose to devote to enjoyment, but which God intends us to devote to suffering. The very beauty, too, of pain itself—the strange flushes of joy that it gives us, which can only thus be won—the certainty that this is reality, this is what we are meant to do and be—happiness of different kinds, art, friends, books, are delusive; they play over the surface; in suffering we dip below it." This latter thought expanded is the subject of a passage of a letter to myself that gave me wonderful comfort.

We know how sickness or sorrow comes down heavily on us, crushing in what we are pleased to call our "plans," and "interrupting," as we say, "our opportunities for usefulness," spoiling our life.

"My dear friend, *this is* life itself. It is this very 'interruption' that we live for. What does God care about the wretched books you intend to write, the petty occupations you think you discharge so gracefully? He means to teach you a great high truth, worth knowing; and, thank Heaven, He will, however much you shrink and writhe. Do not pick and choose among events: try and interpret each as it comes."

At the expiration of the year of work—Easter, 1875—he was unchanged in his plan of travel; in fact, it had become a resolve by that time. He confessed that he did not personally at all like giving up the school work; he had got very much interested in some of the boys, and in the whole process of the education of character. But there was also another reason, which the following letter will explain:

"You know, perhaps, that I have been acting as usher here for a year; it is to be a kind of probation. That is to say, I have promised to try what it is like for a year, and see if I feel inclined to adopt it as my profession.

"Now, I am in a very curious position. I do feel inclined, very much inclined indeed, to stick permanently to the work; it interests, amuses, occupies me. I hate the want of occupation. I hate making occupations for myself, and this provides me with regular work at stated hours, leaving other stated hours free, and free in the best way; that is to say, it works the vapours off. My brain feels clear and steady; I can talk, think, write, read better, in those intervals than I ever can when all my time is my own, and yet—I must, I believe, give it up.

"You know I pretend to a kind of familiar; like Socrates, I am forbidden to do certain things by a kind of distant inward voice—not conscience, for it is not limited to moral choice. I don't mean to say I do not or have not disobeyed it, but it is always the worse for me in the end; it is like taking a short cut in the mountains; you get to your end in time, but far more tired and shaky than if you had followed the right road, which started so much to the left among the pines, and moreover, you get there very much behind your party.

"This time it tells me that I am not equal to the direct responsibility; that I can not, with my habits of mind and temper, impress a permanent enough mark upon the lads. It is like beginning a system of education that is to take, say, thirty years, giving them a year of it, and then taking to another; you not only lose your year, but you unfit them for other systems. That is what I should do; my methods do not prepare them for other normal education; it is only the beginning of a preparation for what I believe to be a higher and more complete education, but that wouldn't justify my keeping on.

"I do not believe that I have done any harm; in fact, my theory would forbid me to think so; but it also informs me that my *rôle* is not to be that of a schoolmaster.

"I shall be a poor man, of course; poor, that is, for an independent gentleman. I wish I were a Fellow of a College at Cambridge; I would try and be as ideal as Gray in that position."

CHAPTER V

In April he was released from his engagement, and he immediately went abroad, alone. He travelled through Normandy into Brittany, spending two months at a little village called Chanteuil, not far from the Point du Sillon. Here he wandered about mostly alone, dressed in the roughest possible costume, and allowing his beard to grow. "At Chanteuil I first learnt how to think, or rather how to converse with myself as I had before done with other persons; I also found for the first time that I did not dislike my own company."

In June he went south, sailing from Brest to Bordeaux, and then descending by land into Spain, where he remained till August. Here he spent a long time in exploring the table-land between the Asturian Mountains and the sea, and then from Burgos visiting Madrid, Toledo, Ciudad, and Seville, and so to Gibraltar. From Gibraltar he sailed up the south-east coast, and settled himself for another month at a little village called Benigarcia, about five miles east of Sorrion, on the river Mijares. In November he sailed by Minorca, starting from Barcelona, to Sicily, and spent the rest of the year in the north of Italy, sailing from Sicily to Genoa, and settling at a village called Riviglio, not very far from Verona. He was obliged to adopt this plan of settling, as his exchequer was not large. From this place he visited Venice on foot, and early in the year visited Rome and Florence, sailing from Ancona in March for Spalatro, and worked up through Hungary to a little place called Bochnia, on the Vistula, down which river he went by boat to Königsberg, staying in Warsaw a few weeks. Once on the Baltic, he hired a fishing-boat, and spent a month in cruising about, during which time he discovered, or rather unearthed, an island, which formed the subject of the only letter he wrote to me during his entire absence.

"Copenhagen, June, 1876.

"My dear Carr,

"I am writing this on board the fishing-smack *Paradys*, which is at this moment lying in Copenhagen Roads, being myself owner by hire and supercargo of the same. The first object of my note is to assure you of my existence, as your letter which was forwarded after me to Danzig seemed to imply uncertainty on that point, and moreover expressed a strange solicitude as to my well-being which was by no means unpleasing to me; then to request you to perform several small commissions for me....

"Lastly, to tell you of a very curious adventure I met with. Some weeks ago I was cruising not very far from Danzig, when we sighted a low wooded island about seven miles off land. I discovered by dint of arduous questioning, for the lingo of these fellows is very uncouth, that it was uninhabited, because its owner, a Danish nobleman, devoted it to the growing of wood for firewood, etc.; a poor speculation, I should say, as the wind blows very fresh from the sea and stunts the trees; and also partly because of a bad name attaching to it, and many horrid superstitions—what, they could not tell me. It was a curious-looking place, not very large, but with deep indented bays all round running very far inland, so as to give it somewhat the shape of a starfish with seven or eight irregular arms; the woods come down very close to the sea and are mostly fir or larch. I could see a few trees further inland of a lighter green, but could not make out to what species they belonged. Between the woods and the sea there are sands loosely overgrown with that spiky grass that covers sand-hills, and at the extremity of two of the valleys a marsh formed by a freshwater spring. The place is frequented by birds, mostly pigeons, and a good many waterfowl of different kinds.

"We spent a hot oppressive day with very little wind in cruising leisurely round it as close in shore as we could get. I should guess that it was about eleven miles round, measuring from the ends of the promontories. We saw no signs whatever of habitation except the three or four old boats on props in one of the creeks used by the woodcutters as cabins when they come. I found out from my men that so great was the horror of the place, that even smugglers, when hard pressed, have been known to risk capture rather than put in to the island; and on my inquiring the cause of these rumours, they gave me various vague and grotesque stories about dead men and women, and a figure which sat on the seaward cape and wept, with long hair drooping all over her; and, worst of all, of two boys, dressed in an antique dress, whom to see was certain disaster, and to speak with certain death.

"Toward evening the breeze freshened; and as it was getting dark I proposed casting anchor in one of the creeks. My men manifested the greatest alarm; but as the channel is full of shoals and sands between the island and the mainland (which is at that place very much deserted), and we were not acquainted with the lie of them, and as I bound myself by the most solemn promises not to send any of them ashore, they at last reluctantly consented. However, as none of them would stir an inch, but crowded together in the most disgusting proximity into their hole of a cabin, I was left the sole patrol of the place.

"It was an oppressive evening, and I walked about a long time up and down, and finally sat down to smoke. The place was curiously silent, except that every now and then it was broken by those strange woodland sounds, like smothered cries or groans, seeming to proceed out of the heart of the wood at a great distance. We lay in a sandy creek with banks of pines on each side, rising up very black against the sky, which had that still green enamelled look that it gets on a very quiet evening. At the far end of the creek was a large marsh covered with the white cotton rush then in bloom; it caused a strange glimmering which I could see till it got quite dark. The only other sound was the wash of the short waves on the sands outside, and the gurgle and cluck of the water as it crept past the boat and out to sea.

"Toward midnight I saw a sight that I have never seen before nor expect to see again. I was surprised to see a light, apparently on the shore, in the direction of the marsh. It looked exactly like a lantern carried by a man. It was very indistinct, but wavered about, always floating about a foot or two from the surface, sometimes standing still as though he was looking for something on the ground, and sometimes moving very quickly. It was a will-o'-the-wisp—a phosphorescent exhalation.

"It was a foul pestilential place, there is no doubt. The mist was all about us by midnight, and smelt very heavy and cold. I awoke shivering in the morning, and not feeling by any means as fresh or vigorous as usual; but nevertheless I determined to explore the island—singly, if none of the men would accompany me.

"Straight up in front of me, apparently about a mile inland, was a very marked clump of trees projecting above the other foliage. I had noticed it several times from the sea the day before. You could see the red stems clearly above the other trees. It evidently marked a knoll or rising ground of some kind, and I determined to make that the object of my journey, and scale, if possible, the trees to get a bird's-eye view of the place.

"As I had expected, I could not get a single member of the crew to accompany me further than the shore, and they were frightened at that. Two of them, who were very much attached to me, implored me most earnestly not to go, but seeing that I was bent upon it, shrugged their shoulders and were silent. The instant I was deposited with my gun on shore, they turned back to the boat and immured themselves. I arranged that at twelve o'clock, if I did not return, they should leave the creek and go round the island within hailing distance, so as to pick me up at any point. I started along the shore, skirting the marsh which wound through the pines.

"The first thing that I came upon was a heronry. I had noticed several of these magnificent birds the day before sailing over the island, and this creek was evidently their settlement; up they went, floating away in all directions with a marvellous, almost magical rapidity and silence of flight. This persuaded me more than anything else that the island was unfrequented, as they are a very shy bird, and distrustful of human beings. I then left the stream and struck straight up into the woods, as nearly as possible toward the clump.

"I put up a few rabbits and a great many pigeons. I also saw an animal that I believe to have been a wolf, but it retreated with such rapidity that I lost sight of it among the tree stems. There was very little undergrowth, as often happens under pines, but the boughs overhead formed a close screen, and the heat was very oppressive. After about an hour's walking I emerged on a cliff above the sea, having mistaken my direction, and crossed the island diagonally. On getting clear of the trees I could again see the goal of my walk, the clump, this time a good deal nearer; and now resolutely plunging into the wood, and keeping always slightly to the right, for I saw that my bias was to the left, I came at last to a place where I could see the sides of a mound through the trees rather indistinctly.

"All of a sudden I came to a low wall among the trees, overgrown in some places, but opposite me almost entirely clear. It was built of large stones carefully fitted together, like the architecture that I remembered to have seen called Cyclopean in architectural histories of Greece. It was easily climbed, and I saw that it surrounded the mound at the distance of about fifty yards, in an irregular circle.

"The space which intervened between it and the mound was partially filled with great hewn stones planted all about, some of them lying on their side, some upright, many of them broken. Going through these I came upon the mound itself. It was crowned with a group of firs, which I could see at once to be much older than the surrounding trees. They were far larger and taller, for the height of the mound did not entirely account for the extraordinary way in which they overtopped the rest of the trees. The mound was very steep, and was apparently constructed of stones built carefully together; but only very small portions of the masonry were visible, it was so overgrown and hidden.

"Wandering round it I found a rude flight of steps leading to the top, also much overgrown. I ascended hastily, and found myself on the top of a smooth plateau, about fifty by thirty yards, surrounded by the gigantic firs; but what immediately arrested my attention was a strange rude altar in the middle, ornamented with uncouth figures and other ornaments. It was covered with moss at the top, and very much cracked and splintered in places.

"I concluded at once that I was in the presence of some remains, probably Druidic in origin, which, owing to the extraordinary desolation of the spot and the superstition attaching to the island, had been so long unvisited as to have been forgotten. I could see that the mound was quite surrounded by the wall, and that it was evidently a sacred enclosure of some kind.

"And gazing and wondering, the stories attributed to the place seemed not wholly without cause. There are certain atmospheres, I have always held, which, as it were, infect one; the very air has caught some contagion of evil which can not be got rid of. There is a baneful influence about some places which makes itself felt upon all sensitive beings who approach. I have felt it on actual battle-fields, as well as at other places that I have held to be the scenes of unrecorded, immemorial slaughters; and as I gazed round it seemed to gather and fall on me here. The very stillness was appalling, for there was now a good deal of wind blowing from the sea, as I could tell from the rustling and cracking of the fir boughs all about, and the sound of the sea on the sand; but here there was an oppressive heaviness, as if the place was still brooding over the ancient horror it had seen. And this was succeeded in my mind by a strange, overpowering, fascinating wonder and speculation as to what dismal deeds of darkness could have been done in the place; with whose blood, indeed, whether of innocent sheep and goats, or pleading men and frightened children, that grim uncouth altar had run and smoked; whether, in truth, as the ancient tales say, every one of those gray pillars all about had been set up, and still was based upon, the mouldering crushed remains of men. The sickening contagion of the sin of the place grew upon me every moment.

"To rid myself of it I applied myself to climb one of the trees to get a bird's-eye view of the island. This I effected without much difficulty, and found that it was of the shape, as I have said, of an irregular five-pointed star. From extremity to extremity, it must be, I believe, about five miles.

"But now follows the part of my story that I do not profess to explain. I marked in my mind the nearest path to the sea, which was to the north-east—the path I actually pursued—and descended; and then

I became aware that the feeling I had experienced before was not purely physical—that there *was* a taint of a real kind in the air, which strangely affected the emotional atmosphere. I felt helpless, bewildered, sickened. I descended, however, from the platform, and walked straight, in what I had determined to be the right direction, when, just as I was about to scale the wall, heartily glad to be out of the place, I was—not exactly called, for there was no sound—but most unmistakably ordered to look round. Am I clear? The sensation produced mentally and emotionally was precisely like the receiving an imperative order that one has neither power nor inclination to resist—so strong and sudden that I kept thinking that my name had been called. In reflecting, however, I am certain that it was not.

"I turned at once, and saw, standing together, close by the platform, two boys, about twelve years of age I should have said, in a loose antique dress, of a bluish-white colour, reaching down to the knees, and girt about the waist, with leather buskins fastened by straps reaching up the leg; their heads were bare, and their hair, which was a dark brown, was loose and flowing. I could not clearly distinguish their faces, but they looked handsome, though desperately frightened. Accompanying this was an indescribable sense, which I have sometimes had in dreams, of an overwhelming intense vastness—space-immensity rushing over one with a terrible power; and at the same time the feeling of *numbers*, as if I was in the presence of a multitude of people. All this quite momentary; in an instant I was conscious of the tall avenues of red stems, with their dark background, and the heavy silence of the underwood, and nothing more.

"I went as if dazed through the wood, yet unconsciously obeying the tacit order of my determination, down a steep fully clad with pine trees, the needles very soft under my feet, till I suddenly came out of the stifling wood on to golden sands and blue water, and a great restful wash of air and sunlight.

"I fired my gun as a signal, and wandering on, as if only half awake, I came out upon another point, and saw the boat lying close below me, whereupon I fired again, and was taken on board.

"My sensation was one of strange languor and fatigue; certainly no fright, and very little wonder; rather as if I had been stunned or charmed by opiates into a kind of waking slumber. I have never felt anything like it before or since.

"But by morning I was shivering in an ague caught in that pestilential fever-swamp, and then the fever fiend himself came and took up his abode with me, and I am now only just convalescent, and can sun myself on the deck, and read and write a little; but the illness and the unconsciousness have done as such things often do—interposed a sort of blank between me and my past life—have deadened it, as one deadens sound by wool, so that memories no longer strike on my mind sharp and clear, but swim along hazy and undefined; and especially is it the case with later memories.

"What was the sight, my dear Carr, that I saw on that hill-top? Was it nothing but the uneasiness of mind and memory disturbed and disorganized by the seething of the foul poison-wine, throwing up pictures and ideas out of their due course, and without subordination to the master-will? Was it merely the story of those fisher-folk, half apprehended, and yet evoked and subtly clad with form and shape by the strange workshop of imagination?

"To all of these I am quite content to say 'Yes.' The sight does not trouble me, or, indeed, anything but interest me. I am not superstitious; I am not nervous in the least. Only I can not help feeling as if, catching, in my weakened state, the hideous leprosy of the place, I had received into my mind, then less able than usual to resist, the stamp and impress of some other mind forced to linger near that spot, and unable to avoid brooding over some haunting remorseful thought or image of a deed, ever dismally recalling how he stood in grim silence watching the tears and prayers of the two soft-faced smooth-limbed Roman boys, kidnapped from some sunny Italian villa, and carried to that gloomy place—held them pitilessly on the altar among the other fork-bearded Druids, with their white robes and glaring eyes—and smote the cruel blow, in spite of the trembling touch of the young fingers and the piteous entreaties, as they looked tearfully from side to side in the damp sunless Golgotha, among the glens of that sinister isle.

"That is the picture that somehow or other, even in my most material mood, is evoked by the thought of the place. The rationalist explanation of the coming fever is far more satisfactory and scientific; but the other keeps recurring—a curious experience anyhow.

"If you have nothing to do you might write me a line to Stockholm, Poste Restante. I am going north to have a look at the ice. Altogether, what with the East still open before me, I do not expect to come home for two or three years.

"You are one of the few friends I can rely upon, so I carry about with me a letter addressed to you; in case of my death you will be the first to be notified of the fact.

"Ever yours,
"Arthur Hamilton."

I have given this letter in full, because it affords a good example of Arthur's descriptive style, which always struck me as being vivid and graphic, and also because this little incident, not by the proof it itself afforded, but by the turn it gave his thoughts—then rather rapidly drifting into materialism—was the first step in a kind of conversion from the purely physical views of life he had been apt to take. The episode itself, too, is a curious one, and may deserve to be recorded.

CHAPTER VI

Nothing is more hopelessly wearisome than descriptions of travel; even George Eliot could not make in her diaries Florence anything but dull. I shall confine myself to sketching his route, to telling one incident among the few he told me, and describing his return.

I had no more letters from him; but he has told me that he got to Spitzbergen, and in a whaler to the edge of the great arctic ice-field. He sailed to America and crossed it. From San Francisco he visited Peru and the Amazon, on which river he spent a month. Then he went to Africa, to what part I do not know, except that he came down the Nile; and then he wandered through Asia Minor, Persia, and India; he penetrated a little way into Thibet, and saw China and Japan; he went up to the mouth of the Siberian rivers, travelling for three months with a party of gipsies, who taught him many curious things, such as their own language and freemasonry, the use of simples, the properties of water, and the strange things that can be done with even such things as docks and nettles, and other plants which we toss away as weeds. He told me that in that branch of secret knowledge, as in all others, there was a vast deal of nonsense but a solid residuum of truth; and he said, half jestingly, that they had sworn him a member of their brotherhood, and what was more, he had since discovered many members of the brotherhood in civilized nations, even in "kings' houses."

But I must suspend my account for a short time to relate the incident to which I have just referred. It took place during his stay in Teheran, while on his way home (1878), a period of about six weeks. This city is situated in a lovely climate—hot, but not unbearable for Europeans; houses, horses, and servants are extraordinarily cheap. The house that Arthur took was situated in large gardens or pleasure-grounds of the natural wilderness type that one finds in the East, shrubberies relegated to certain limits, but within those limits left absolutely to their own device and will, with the exception of arched and shaded paths cut under the thick intertwined leafage.

This whole place, with horses at his command, and seven servants, with the whole expense of boarding, cost him, he has told me, £40 for the entire six weeks that he was there; for he was very weary of his rough tramping life, and resolutely determined to recruit his energies by some deliberate luxury, a recipe far more useful than the normal Englishman is at all inclined to admit, thinking, as he does so erroneously, that "overtasking the body is the best restorative for the overworked mind, and *vice versâ*," as Arthur said once, "whereas the two instruments, so to speak, have but one blade though two handles."

The heat of the day was rather overpowering; that period he usually spent dozing or reading in the court of the house, which was occupied by a cool flashing fountain in the centre of an oasis of marble pavement, streaked and veined. About seven it became cooler, and then in the light native costume he used to ride leisurely about the picturesque city or among the delightful houses scattered about in the outskirts like his own.

One evening he was riding in this fashion down a lane running between high brick walls, fringed with feathery trailing shrubs or gorgeous red and white flowers, whose fragrance literally streamed into the evening air, in that delicate dusk when the senses are lulled into acquiescence, and the mind and emotions become so vivid and lustrous in their play.

Riding along with his eyes half closed and lost in a delicious reverie, his horse turned of its own accord to the left, and went for some distance up an embowered road; Arthur suddenly roused himself to find that he was passing close to a large sombre house, that had evidently once been fortified, looming very impressively in the languorous air; the gate had been opened for some purpose and not closed again, and he was, in fact, trespassing in some private grounds.

He checked his horse, looking curiously about him, and was just about to return when he heard a voice apparently proceeding from the centre of one of the shrubberies, asking him his business in Persian. Looking in that direction he managed to distinguish two or three indistinct figures seated on a low seat on a kind of terrace on his left.

He rode up, and mustering up the little Persian he possessed, apologized for his unintentional intrusion, mingling a good deal of English, as he said, with his rather incoherent explanation.

He was aware that one of the figures disengaged itself from the group, and coming up close to him, regarded him with some curiosity. It was a tall man, paler in complexion than the natives are wont to be, with large dreamy eyes, and an air of indifferent lassitude that was rather fascinating.

He was amazed to hear, at the conclusion of his lame peroration, a voice of strange delicacy of intonation proceeding from the figure: "An Englishman, I presume." The accent was a little affected, but the speaker was evidently more English than Persian by training: "Not only English," said Arthur to himself, "but London English of the best kind."

He confessed his nationality, and, again apologizing, was about to withdraw, when the stranger courteously invited him to join the party. "It is very refreshing," he said, "to hear my native tongue by chance; I can not resist the temptation of begging you to join us for a little, that I may hear it once more; you will do me a great kindness if you will accede to my request."

Seeing that the offer was sincere, Arthur dismounted, and walked to the terrace with the other. The figures rose at their approach, and Arthur could see that they were two boys of fifteen or sixteen, of extraordinary beauty and delicacy, and a woman of about thirty-five, as far as he could judge, evidently their mother.

His host spoke a few words in Persian, the purport of which he could not catch, and, rapidly presenting him, requested him to be seated, and produced some cigarettes of a very choice and fragrant kind.

They talked for a long time on general subjects—England, politics, art, and literature. The stranger seemed well acquainted with literature and events of a certain date, but not of later departures in any branch; and finally, Arthur gave a short account of himself and his wanderings, in which the others appeared most interested.

Before he went back to his house the stranger asked him, with some earnestness, to return on the following day, which Arthur gladly accepted. One of the boys conducted him to the gate, speaking a few English sentences with that delicate and hesitating utterance that combines with other personal attractions to give an almost unique charm.

On the following day, and on several others, the invitation was repeated and accepted. The stranger became more communicative, having at first consistently maintained a courteous reserve.

The last day of Arthur's stay in his villa he went to see his new friends. The boys had taken a great fancy to him, and used to wait for his coming at the gate; but they would never come to his house, though he asked them more than once. They were not permitted, they said, to leave their own domain.

On this last evening his host was alone, and after some indifferent conversation he told Arthur the following story, and made a proposal which had a strange influence on the rest of his life:

"You may have wondered," he said, "at the cause which brought me here, and keeps me here. I have often admired your courtesy, which has made no attempts to discover my antecedents; it is not the usual characteristic of our nation. If you are disposed to hear, I am willing to give you a little autobiographical outline, which is a necessary preface to a request which I am going to make of you."

He then mentioned his name and parentage—facts which I am not at liberty to repeat. They surprised even Arthur when he heard them; they surprised me, when he communicated them to me, even more.

He was the son of an English nobleman of high rank and wealth and aristocratic traditions, and was reported to be long since dead. Many people will no doubt remember the shock which the news of the premature death of this individual, when announced in Europe, made. It took place at Palermo in 1853. More than that I am not at liberty to state.

"My reasons for this were as follows," said his host. "I meditated a retirement from the world of a kind which should be absolute, which should excite no inquiries, no interest, except a retrospective one. To have merely disappeared would not have suited my purpose; search would have been instituted. The connections and influence of my family would have made such a plan liable to constant disaster. From Palermo, after superintending the making of my tombstone, I came straight back here, to a house which I had already prepared for myself under an anonymous name. I travelled with the utmost secrecy; I married, as you have seen, a native wife; and from that day to this I have never beheld a European face but yours. Your arrival was so unexpected as to shiver resolve and habit; but I have no reason to regret, as far as I can see, my confidence. I feel that I can unreservedly trust you.

"You will no doubt wonder as to my aim in executing this hazardous and Quixotic project. I do not mind telling you now, at this lapse of time, though I have never before opened my reasons to any one, because I think that I observe in you traces of that temper which led me to take the step.

"It seemed to me that Western life had got into a confusion and complication from which nothing could deliver it. The principles now incorporated with the very existence of the most influential men in it seemed to me to be radically erroneous, and the disposition of the Western mind is of a kind which augments with indefinite rapidity the strength of any prevalent idea.

"What I mean is this. May I explain by a quotation? A sentence from a certain review of the poet Coleridge's life and work is as follows: 'Devoted as he was to mystic and ideal contemplation, to abstractions of mind and spirit, he naturally became untrustworthy in every relation of life.'

"That represents, in an exaggerated form, the ideal of the Western mind. They are, though they would not so name themselves, gross materialists; and the tendency is increasing on them daily and yearly. Those who protest occasionally against current thought, who appear like prophets with bitter invective and words of warning on their lips, are swept away by the tide, and write of trade and treaties, of wars of principle and convenience. The very divines are tainted. 'Live your life to the uttermost,' they cry.

"And in the Western mind the tendency once rooted gathers force from every quarter. As a necessary concomitant of the restless habit, the enshrining of the 'effective man' in their proudest temples, comes an extreme deference to other people, a heated straining of the ears to catch the murmurs of that vague uncertain heart—Public Opinion. And why? It follows: if it is in this life alone that triumphs must be won—if on this stage alone the drama is to be played out, and the time is short—it is that imperious will that you must conciliate; therefore employ every power to gain the art of so doing.

"So intent are the Westerns on this drama, so wrapped up in the actors, so anxious to declaim and strut, that they forget to what end the play exists: they have left the spectators out for whom alone the scenes are enacted, and who, though apparently so silent and motionless, are the *raison d'être* of the whole performance. The play must and will continue through the ages; but the wise, the enlightened, beat down, and in one sharp encounter overcome, the lower desire of being seen and applauded, and are content to sit and watch—the nobler task.

"For we must remember that it is not the drama itself, tragedy or comedy, fascinating as it be, that we are here to watch—but the mind of the Being that animates the whole, can be here descried and here alone, as in a mirror faintly: it is not only the man who fumes and paces up and down for a few moments and then is called away; but the vast Existence behind, that knows what the play means and will not tell us, and that pushes the players on and off as He will.

"And here we find ourselves, with our tiny and uncertain space of time bounded by the Infinities at either end, with the huge puzzle set before us. A method has been invented, is now traditional, of closing the eyes easily and thoughtlessly to the whole; and we are content to catch that contagion from our predecessors: we eat and drink, we work and play, and stifle the restless questioning that springs up so resolutely in our spaces of solitude here; and what will it do in the immeasurable hereafter?

"When I lived in England I was for a short time the member of a professional circle of men engaged on high educational aims. They held, so far as any teachers can be said to hold, many futures in their hands. We know that lives teach more than words; and how did these men set themselves to live?

"First, to perform their work with rigid accuracy: I will do them justice — to do it *perfectly*; but granted that, as speedily as possible: and, their work over, to amuse themselves — literally: to play games that they enjoyed with childish keenness, and fill up all the day with them; to read the papers; to play whist; to smoke in the sun; to get through a certain amount of general reading for conversational purposes, and to gossip about one another and their doings, and talk about their work, in which, it must be confessed, they were enthusiastically interested, only in a gossipy detailed way, amassing incident rather than arriving at principles. There was only one who was engaged in serious work of a kind involving scientific research, and he forfeited much of his doctrinal and all his social influence thereby; 'A man should stick to his work,' they said, 'not pretend to do one thing while he is thinking about another.'

"A low ideal, faithfully carried out, is the most effective; not because the high ideal is high, but because so few are capable of carrying it out; and in that Western world success in aims proposed is the highest that a man can aspire to.

"And suppose we do make ourselves famous, what then? how do we use our fame? To make life happier? It might be so, but is it? No, for ordinary minds the strain is too strong. 'I will gain fame,' the pure young soul said once, 'as an engine of power, that I may have a platform where men will listen to me;' but the effort of struggling thither has been too much, and once arrived there, what is his object now? merely to remain there, and among the crowd of pushing selfish figures, that have lost in the fight the very signs of their humanity, *monstrari digito*, to have the gaze of men, to feel somebody.

"All this I throw aside, and go straight to God. All around us in natural things — in the curve of that rose-stem and the passionate flush of its petals — in those white bells there, looking as if blown out of veined foam — in the luscious scents that wind and linger round the garden, He has set, as in a language, the secrets of His being and ours, of our why and wherefore, if we could but read them. Like the characters and monuments of a bygone age staring from a waste of sand or the front of a precipice, these words and phrases seem to say, not 'There was a king who was mighty, but whose throne is cut down,' but 'There lives a God who would be all tenderness if He could, and is more beautiful in His nature than anything you have ever seen or dreamed of. Win your way to Him, if you can; do not let Him go till you have His secret. That is a talisman indeed, that shall shut you in palaces of delight where no torment shall touch you.'

"And not a selfish paradise. We are but as others, we mystics; it is only that we take—or rather are led, for it is no will of ours, but an imperious voice that calls us—the straight and flowery road to God, pressing through but one hedge of thorns, while you and others struggle to Him along the dusty road that winds and wanders. But our paradise would be no paradise if we did not know that our brothers were coming, coming; the beauty that we behold, sheer ugliness if we did not believe that you will some day share it too.

"Yes, I am a mystic—have joined the one brotherhood that is eternal and all-embracing, as young as love and as old as time—the society that no man suspects till he is close upon it, or hopes to enter till he finds himself in a moment within the sacred pale. I would that I could tell you with what different eyes we look on life and death, God and nature, from this divine vantage-ground on which we stand, and you would imperil all, run through fire and water, to win it too; but you must find the way yourself—no man can show it you. If you enter—and you are destined to enter this side the grave—it will come when you are least expecting it. In the middle of those that cry 'Lo, here is Christ and there,' He himself will touch you on the shoulder, and show you better things than these.

"Oh, if I could only help you there at once—open the door! But my words would bear other and commoner meanings in your ear; if I opened the door, you would not see the light. Ay, and I do not wish it; for every step outside you take is apportioned you; you need them, that you may appreciate, when you have it, the rest within.

"And now for my request. You need not answer now; you may have a year to think of it.

"You have seen my two boys. Outwardly they are alike, inwardly very different—that you could not see.

"The younger will join me soon; he is far advanced upon the way already, though he little suspects it. I have no fears for him. God is drawing him.

"But the elder—like as he is in face, form, disposition—will need another discipline. He must tread the winding road, the road of other men. His trial will be a sharp one; through many paths he will have to be taught the truth. I could hardly bear it, when I look at the tender face, the dreamy eyes, and feel his caressing hand, thinking of the horrors he must look upon, if I did not know that all will be well.

"Will you undertake a charge for me? I could not play a part in the world again, even if I would. I have lost my hold on men. I do not realize what are their hopes and fears, their ideals, and most of all, their whims and caprices; and, what is more, I could never appreciate them now. Ten years' isolation is enough to spoil one for that; in ten years many social traditions and commonplaces of life have changed. I should have to ask the reasons for many things. I should never feel them instinctively, as those do who have grown old along with them.

"And so I can not undertake the task of guiding him in this harsh world that he must enter. I have known, however, for some time that it would be undertaken and accomplished for me. You have been sent to me, later than I thought, but still sent. I have been waiting; I have been true to my creed, and have not been impatient.

"I intrust him to you as I intrust the fairest possession I have, knowing that you will feel the responsibility. You will find him passionately affectionate, and in danger there; quick to anger, and in danger there; personally fascinating and beautiful, and in danger there; and in these three things his trial will be. But he does not resent nor brood; he is docile, apt to listen, eager to comprehend; and he is truthful and sincere."

I have given this in a continuous speech, much as Arthur told it me a few months ago, though it was the essence of a conversation. The quiet man, with his dreamy eyes fixed on his face, he told me, and the fragrant Eastern garden seemed from moment to moment of the strange adventure to swim and become vague and phantasmal; but again the quiet air of certainty with which questions were asked and statements made gave him a curious sense of security, and an impulse to accept the indicated path, together with a sense of shrinking from such a responsibility.

"I do not, as I told you," said the other, "want your answer now, but this day one year hence, August 19, 1879, I shall claim it. And I have no doubt," he added with a smile, "of what that answer will be. But I beg of you do not give the question a hasty consideration and then reverse your decision. Do not attempt to decide. Let your choice be guided by circumstances; they are the safest guide, for they are not of our own making.

"I do not suppose," he continued, "that I shall ever see you again on earth, as you proceed with your journey to-morrow; and indeed I think it will perhaps be as well that this should be our last conversation, so that nothing else should interfere to blur the impression.

"One last word then." He paused for a moment, and the stillness was broken only by the faintest stir of odorous wind among the spice-trees and a waft of distant evening noises.

"You are treading a path, though you do not realize it, which it is not given to many men to tread. You have had your first intimation of the goal to-day, and the future will not be wanting in indications of the same; but, as I have said, you will suddenly, when you least expect it, step inside the circle, and everything will be changed.

"To you I wish to intrust a future that I can not mould myself, to be moulded, not for me, but for the great Master of all. You are the chosen instrument for this. My work lies in another region, which you will realize on that day when all things are made plain.

"Only remember that your destiny is high and arduous, and that a single false step may throw you from a precipice that has taken years to scale once, and that must be scaled again. For you walk among the clouds, or very near them; you are not defiled by any gross habitual sin; your heart is pure, and you have known suffering. You are a true novice.

"In a year, as I have said, I shall claim your answer. And now farewell for a season. When we next meet we shall have a larger common ground; we shall be master and pupil no longer.

"You shall see the boy once again, by his wish and my own. He shall go with you to your house to-night, and travel with you the first stage to-morrow. I have arranged for his return."

He then conducted Arthur into the house, where he bade adieu to the mistress and to the younger son; the elder, his charge that was to be, meeting him as he came out, and accompanying him home. The boy had formed a great attachment to him, and the idea of their future relations sent a strange and unwonted glow into Arthur's mind, so that he parted from him on the next day, "with wonder in his heart," and something very like an ache too.

This last episode will appear to my readers to be so fantastic as to give the work at once a fictional character; they will say that on some real lines I have constructed a romance of the wildest type, and that Arthur is no longer an interesting personality, because as a rule he is too ordinary to be ideal, in the last two chapters too illusory to be real.

All I can urge is this: the chapters shall be their own defence. If I had wished to present my readers with nothing but a dry chronicle of facts I should have toned this down to something more prosaic. But every one who has had any experience of life will know that her surprises are sometimes very bewildering; that fiction is nothing but uncommon experience made ordinary, or heaped inartistically upon a single character.

It may be said that the man was mentally affected, in the latter scene; in the former, that Arthur himself was the victim of a mental disorder; but he left such vivid and detailed descriptions of both events that I have been enabled to give one (the letter) exactly as it stands, and the interview in Teheran is taken directly from diaries—a little amplified and reconstructed, it is true, but only when interpreted by the light of later events.

And this must be always the task of the true biographer; for the biographer has to take a life *en masse*, and disentangling the predominant and central threads, cast the rest away; in this process rejecting facts and incidents whose isolated interest is often greater than the interest of what he retains, because it is on the latter that the pearls of life are, so to speak, strung.

In this case the two incidents I have kept are both so pregnant of influence upon his later life, so necessary to the logical development of his principles, that, in spite of their romantic, not to say wild, character, I have retained them.

CHAPTER VII

About the middle of February, 1879, I was sitting at work in my lodgings in Newman Street, when I was interrupted by the advent of my landlady, to inform me that there was a gentleman below who wished to see me. I told her to show him up, and she returned in a moment, ushering in, to my extreme surprise, Arthur Hamilton. I confess I hardly knew him at first. He had grown a beard, and looked thinner and graver than he used to do. He had the same slow, almost stately movement, with a slight and not ungraceful suggestion of languor; his manner was somewhat changed, and very much improved; and he had contracted, from living so long with strangers, a delightfully frank and free way of speaking. He never gave me, as he used to, the least feeling of constraint; he always seemed perfectly at his ease. And he had acquired, too, the art of asking unobtrusive questions of a tentative kind, so as to feel out the interests of his companion, and draw him out; not in that professional way which so-called influential people often acquire—the melancholy confidential smile, the intimate manner, and the air of bland inattention with which they receive your remarks, only to be detected in the fixed or wandering eye. He had learnt the art of being interested in other people, and in what they had to say, and of indicating by a subtle tact in speech that he was following them, and intelligently sympathizing with them.

He did not then tell me much about himself. He confessed that the most rapturous feeling he had known since he set off on his travels, was the hour or two as he whirled through the flat pasture-lands and the pleasant green of Kent.

He gave me no detailed descriptions of adventures, but hinted in a suggestive way that he had seen much, and thought more. "I think I have learnt myself very fairly," was the only remark he made about his own personal experience.

"To finish my tour," he said, "I want to see something of my native land. I have been away so long, that I don't know where to begin, and I want you to help me. I want to be introduced to a few Christian households, that I may see the kind of people that our Western friends are."

I had an uncle, a Mr. Raymond, who had made a fortune in business, lived in a fine house in Lancaster Gate, and saw a good deal of fairly interesting and cultivated people. I took him to dine there once or twice, and he needed nothing else. He had a real genius for *tête-à-tête* conversation; that is, he could listen without appearing only to listen. He made people feel at their best with him. My aunt's criticism of him was highly characteristic of the British matron and her choice of friends.

"I thoroughly approve, Harry," she said to me, "of your friend, Mr. Hamilton. He is very well-informed and clever, and he doesn't allow it to make him in the least disagreeable." And starting from this, he was asked to dinner by, and invited to visit, a fair selection of pleasant people.

Of the events which immediately succeeded his return to England I can not, for two reasons, give a very detailed account. In the first place, dealing as they do with living people, I have thought it better, after consultation with the friends of both, to leave the outlines of the story rather vague; and secondly, there are great gaps and deficiencies in diaries and letters, which, though I believe I can supply, knowing what I do of the circumstances, I hardly like to fill in in a narrative of fact.

He took a dose, as I have already said, of the London season. "Those six weeks," he said, "absolutely knocked me up; my friends told me, among other things, that my physiognomy, being of a grave and gloomy cast, was of a kind that was not suitable to a festive occasion; and so I used to come home at night with my jaws positively aching with the effort of a perpetually fatuous grin."

The following extract, which I have selected from one of his letters of this period, will give a good picture of his mind:

"I think that two of the things that move me most, not to sadness nor indignation, but to those vague tumultuous feelings for which we have, I think, no name, but which were formerly called melancholy, are these:

"To come up-stairs after a hot London banquet, where you have been sitting, talking the poorest trash, between two empty, worldly women; and then, perhaps, listening to stories that are dull, or worse, and see dullness personified in every one of the twelve faces that stare at you with such sodden respectability through the cigarette smoke; and then, I say, to come up-stairs, and see moving about among the knowing selfish people a child with hair like gold thread, and something of the regretful innocence of heaven in her eyes and motions. If you can get her to talk to you, so much the better for you; but if you or she are shy, as generally happens, to watch her is something. God knows the insidious process by which she will be transformed, step by step, into one of those godless fine ladies; for it makes me inclined to pray that anything may happen to her first that may hinder that development.

"The other thing is, under the same circumstances, to sit down and hear some rippling melody of Bach's, a tender gavotte or a delicate rapid fugue, just as it stole on to the paper in that quaint German garden with the clipped yew-hedges and the tall summer-house in the corner, in the master's pointed handwriting, calling down by his magic wand the spirits of the air to aid him in the perfecting of the exquisite phrase that some Ariel had whispered to him as he walked or sat.

"To hear that little rill of Paradise breaking out in the glaring room, not echoed or reflected in the rows of listless faces, gives me a strange turn. It sweeps away for a minute or two, as it goes and comes and returns upon itself until its sweet course is run, all the hard and stifling web of convention and opinion that closes us in; it takes me back for a moment to old-world fancies, till I seem to feel, as I am always longing to feel, that we are separated only by a very little flimsy hedge from the secrets of the beautiful, from the shadow-land which is so real; and that every now and then a breeze breaks and stirs across, with something of the fragrance of the place in its wandering air."

He used to come to me in my rooms in Newman Street, on his way back from an evening party or a ball, to smoke a cigar, and it was very interesting to watch his growing disgust for the life, and the grotesque and humorous ways in which he expressed it.

"Do I feel flat?" he used to say—"it isn't the word—bored to death. Why, my dear Chris, if you'd heard the conversation of the lady next me to-night, you'd have thought that the premier said, every morning when his shaving-water was brought him, 'Another day! Whose happiness can I mar? Whose ruin can I effect? What villainy can I execute to-day?'"

One night, at dinner, he happened to sit next a young lady in whom the fashionable world were a good deal interested.

It is impossible to give a fair sketch of her character; she was what would now be called unconventional, and was then called fast.

She openly avowed her preference for men's society as compared to female—women, as a rule, did not like her—she used to receive calls from her own men friends in her own room whenever she liked, and it was considered rather "compromising" to know her.

She was perfectly reckless about what she said and did. I questioned Arthur about her conversation, for she was accused of telling improper stories. "I have often," he said, "heard her allude to things and tell stories that would be considered unusual, even indelicate. But I never heard her say a thing in which there could be any conceivable 'taint,' in which the point consisted in the violation of the decent sense. The 'doubtful' element was rare and always incidental."

Arthur told me a delightful story about her. Her father was a testy old country gentleman, very irritable and obstinate.

It happened that an Eton boy was staying in the house, of the blundering lumpish type; he had had more than his share of luck in breaking windows and articles of furniture. One morning Mr. B——, finding his study window broken, declared in a paroxysm of rage that the next thing he broke the boy should go.

That same afternoon, it happened he was playing at small cricket with Maud, and made a sharp cut into the great greenhouse. There was a crash of glass, followed by Maud's ringing laugh.

They stopped their game, and went to discuss the position of events. As they stood there, Mr. B——'s garden door, just round the corner, was heard to open and slam, and craunch, craunch, came his stately pace upon the gravel.

They stared with a humorous horror at one another. In an instant, Maud caught up a lawn-tennis racquet that was near, and smashed the next pane to atoms. Mr. B—— quickened his pace, hearing the crash, and came round the corner with his most judicial and infuriated air, rather hoping to pack the culprit out of the place, only to be met by his favourite daughter. "Papa, I'm so sorry, I've broken the greenhouse with my racquet. May I send for Smith? I'll pay him out of my own money."

The Eton boy adored her from that day forth; and so did other people for similar reasons.

I, personally, always rather wondered that Arthur was ever attracted by Miss B——, for he was very fastidious, and the least suggestion of aiming at effect or vulgarity, or hankering after notoriety, would infallibly have disgusted him. But this was the reason.

She was never vulgar, never self-conscious. She acted on each occasion on impulse, never calculating effects, never with reference to other people's opinions.

A gentleman once said, remonstrating with her for driving alone with a Cambridge undergraduate in his dog-cart down to Richmond after a ball, "People are beginning to talk about you."

"What fools they must be!" said Miss B——, and showed not the slightest inclination to hear more of the matter.

There is no question, I think, that Arthur's grave and humorous ways attracted her. He, when at his best, was a racy and paradoxical talker—with that natural tinge of veiled melancholy or cynicism half-suspected which is so fascinating, as seeming to imply a "*past*," a history. He ventured to speak to her more than once about her tendency to "drift." He told me of one conversation in particular.

"I think you have too many friends," he said to her once, at the conclusion of an evening party at her own house. They were sitting in a balcony looking out on to the square, where the trees were stirring in the light morning wind.

"That's curious," she said. "I never feel as if I had enough; I have room enough in my heart for the whole world." And she spread out her hands to the great city with all her lights glaring before them. "God knows I love you all, though I don't know you," she said with a sudden impulse.

They were silent for a moment.

Then she resumed: "Tell me why you said that," she said. "I like to be told the truth."

"*You* may feel large enough," he said, "but they don't appreciate your capacity; they feel hurt and slighted. Why, only to-night, during the ten minutes I was talking to you, you spoke and dismissed eight people, every one of whom was jealous of me, and thinking 'Who's the new man?' And I began to wonder how I should feel if I came here and found a new man installed by you, and got a handshake and a smile."

"Shall I tell you?" she said, looking at him. "I should give you a look which would mean, 'I would give anything to have a quiet talk to you, Mr. Hamilton, but the exigencies of society oblige me to be civil to this person.'"

"Yes," he said, "and that's just what I complain of; it gives me, the new man to-night, a feeling of insecurity—that perhaps you are just 'carrying on' with me because it is your whim, and that the instant I bore you, you will throw me away like a broken toy, and with even less regret."

"How dare you speak like that to me?" she said, turning upon him almost fiercely. "I never forget people." And she rose and went quickly into the room, and didn't speak to him for the rest of the evening.

But just as he was going out he passed her, and hardly looked at her, thinking he had offended her; but she came and put out her hand quickly, and said, almost pathetically—

"You must forgive me for my behaviour to-night, Mr. Hamilton. What you said was not true, but you meant it to be true; you believed it. And please don't stop talking to me openly. I value it very much. I have so few people to tell me the truth."

I find this conversation narrated in his diary, almost word for word as I have given it. But there is omitted from it, necessarily perhaps, the most pregnant comment of all.

"And yet," he said to me once, as he turned to leave the room after commenting upon their freedom of speech with one another, "I am not in love with her, though I can't think why I am not."

The sequel must be soon told. Miss B—— suddenly accepted a gentleman who was in every way a suitable *parti*: heir to a peerage, of fairly high character.

But to return to Arthur. I can not do better than quote a few sentences of a letter he wrote to me on the event. It conceals—as he was wont to do—strong feeling under the bantering tone.

"As you are in possession of most of my moral and mental diagnoses, I had better communicate to you a new and disturbing element. You remember what I said to you about Miss B——, that I did not care for her. A fancied immunity is often a premonitory symptom of disease: the system is excited into an instantaneous glow by the first contact of the poisonous seed.

"I don't know, at present, quite how things are with me. I labour under a great oppression of spirit. I have a strange thirsty longing to see her face and hear her speech. If I could only hear from herself that she had done what her best self—of which we have often spoken—ratifies, I should feel more content. But she trusts her impulses too much; and the habit of loving all she loves with passion, blinds her a little. A woman who loves her sister, her pets, the very sunshine and air with passion, hardly knows what a lover is. I can not help feeling that I might have shown her a little better than J——. Still one must accept facts and interpret them, especially in cases where one has not even been allowed to try and fail; for I never spoke to her a word of love. Ah, well! perhaps I shall be stronger soon."

CHAPTER VIII

Arthur Hamilton as an author

I must give a chapter to this subject, because it entered very largely into Arthur's life, although he was singularly unsuccessful as an author, considering the high level of his mental powers.

He lacked somehow, not exactly the gift of expression—his letters testify to that—but the gift of proportion and combination.

His essays are disjointed—discursive and eloquent in parts, and bare and meagre in others. Connections are omitted, passages of real and rare beauty jostling with long passages of the most common-place rhetoric. His platitudes, however, to myself who knew him, have a genuine ring about them; he never admitted a truism into his writing till it had become his own by vivid realization. As he himself says:

"I always find a peculiar interest in the solemn enunciation of a platitude by a dull person who does not naturally aim at effect. You feel sure it is the condensation of life and experience. Such an utterance often brings a platitude home to me as no amount of rhetorical writing can."

Still, the reading public will not stand this, and Arthur never found a market.

He wrote voluminously.

I have in my bureau several pigeon-holes crammed with manuscripts in his curious sprawling hand. He wrote, when he was in the mood, very quickly, with hardly an erasure. Among them is:

1. A collection of poems (128 in all).

2. A complete novel, called "The Unencumbered Man."

3. Three incomplete novels, called "Physiognomy," "Helena," "From Hall to Hall."

4. Essays on historical and literary subjects, such as "Coleridge," "Bunyan," "The Earl of Surrey," "Lucian," etc. These, as far as I can make out, are very poor.

5. A collection of semi-mystical writings and short stories. There is a great fertility of imagination about these, and they are composed in a very finished style. It is not improbable that I shall re-edit these, as they seem to me to be distinctly first-rate work. I give a short specimen of his mystical writing—a style of which he was very fond. It is called:

"The Great Assize

"Now, it came to pass that on a certain day the Gods were weary. Odin sat upon his throne, and rested his chin upon his hand. And Thor came in, and threw his hammer upon the earth, and said, 'I am weary of walking up and down in the earth, of smiting and slaying; and I know not how to bind or heal up, and I am too old to learn.' And Freya said, 'I am weary of Valhalla and the birds and trees, the perpetual sunshine and the feasts and laughter.' So also said all the Gods.

"And Odin, when the clamour was stilled, rose from his throne, and spoke. He told them of an ancient law of the Gods, so ancient that it seemed dim even to himself, that when the Gods should be heavy and be sad at heart, they should appoint a judgment for men, should open the everlasting records, and call the world to the assize; and Loki should be the accuser, and Night and Day the witnesses, and Odin should deliver sentence, with the Gods for assessors.

"So Thor stepped out upon the bar of heaven, and blew the steel trumpet that is chained to the door-post of the hall.

"Shrill and angry came the sound of the great horn over earth, her woods and valleys; and terrible was the sound of wailing and lamentation. They prayed to the mountains to fall upon them, and the sea to swallow them up; for they said, 'The secrets of the heart must now be spoken. The Lord and our brethren will hear them. And who can bear the shame? Oh, that we had not turned away!'

"But the winds of the earth, and the voices of the morning, and the waves of the moaning sea drove them shrieking into the judgment hall, and Loki began his accusation.

"And so foul a tale it was, that the men and women folk prayed and cried no longer, but sank down in dull silence for fear. And the stars that listened overhead shrank out of the sky, and the sea stilled his waves to hear, and the very Gods turned pale and red where they sat, to think that vileness and oppression had thriven so upon the earth, and that deeds of shame had fallen so thick, and that they had in no wise hindered it, but rather increased the sum of sin.

"At last the words of Loki were over, and left a burning silence in the hall; and the sun and moon bowed their heads in witness, and Night and Day said 'Yea,' and 'Truth, he has told truth.'

"Then there was a silence, and all looked at Odin as he sat, sunk down and silent, in his chair, staring at the shrinking crowd with eyes of shame, and majesty, and anger.

"And at the last he rose, and he was clad in grey mists from head to foot, with a cloud of gleaming gold upon his head, like the sunlight on white cliffs seen over the sea through the haze of a summer morning.

"But ere he opened his lips to speak, one who sat among the folk arose and came up the hall, walking strongly and briskly like a king, and looking about him with a resolute and cheerful face to left and right.

"And all held their breath to see him pass, wondering what this thing might be.

"But the man, when he had reached the middle of the hall, cried with a loud voice, 'Hold.'

"And Odin's face gleamed white with rage through the fringes of the mist, and he said between his teeth, 'Who art thou?'

"And at his voice Freya started and blanched, and wrapped herself in her robe.

"And the man said, in a clear loud voice, not defiant, but with a certain royalty about it—

"'Lord Odin, I am he of whom thou spokest but now; he of whom the ancient oracles have spoken, whom thou knowest, and yet knowest not.'

"And Odin said, 'I know thee not; stand aside therefore, that I may judge thee and thy fellows.'

"And there was a hideous silence for a moment while you might count a score, and the twain stared upon each other.

"Then the man said, in the same voice that shook not nor quivered, 'When the Gods shall sit in order to judge the earth, then shall one come out of the midst of created things, through the earth, and walking upon it; and at his coming the pillars of Valhalla shall be snapped, and the everlasting halls shall fall.' And he added other words, which the Gods knew, but not the men or women folk. And when he ceased speaking there blew as it were a whirlwind out of Valhalla, and the high Gods passed away, as it were in skeins and fringes of hanging mist. Then there were lightnings and thunders, and the earth shook; and terrible voices were heard in heaven, passing to and fro. And one said, 'Hence, ye that corrupt justice;' and another said, 'The brood of the eagle is come home to roost;' and another, 'The roof is down.' And then there were yells and groans; and among mankind there was weeping and laughter, many smiles and tears, and they cried to the stranger, 'Judge us, thou king of Gods and men.' But he, turning, said, 'Nay, but ye are judged already.' Then was there peace on earth."

There are, besides these, several unfinished studies, and two or three note-books full of jotted conversations and thoughts of all kinds—a curious mixture.

He carefully left all the publishers' letters which he received in answer to his application. They are twenty-two in number, and are all refusals. They are tied carefully up, and are labeled, "My Literary Career."

All these compositions are the work of about seven years, except some of the poems which were written at Cambridge. The novel was begun and finished in about six weeks, in 1878. It is a poor plot, and mawkish in character, though not without merits of style.

During all this time his interest in writing never flagged. He felt that he had one or two ideas, on which he had a firm grasp, to communicate to the world, and he worked at them incessantly in new and ever-varying forms.

The issue would seem to show that he was not destined to communicate them directly to others—at least, in his own lifetime; and, indeed, no one was quicker at interpreting events than himself. He gave the enterprise a long and severe trial, but the resolute front with which he was met, showed him clearly that it was not to be. It may be that the record of his life, little as he ever imagined it would come before the world, may effect a part of what he himself prepared to do.

Occasionally, for he was of quick sensibilities, throughout this period he felt the bitterness of constant rebuff. The following letter he wrote me shows it:

"I am beginning to feel as if publishers had a code of signals or private marks like freemasonry, which they scribble sometimes, like the concealed marks on bank-notes, on the first page of a manuscript, so as to spare their brother publishers the trouble of looking through a manuscript which is below market value. I have never had a manuscript accepted which has been once refused; and I now eagerly scan the first page, to see if I can discover a wriggling mark in the margin or among the lines which is to tell Smith and Co. that Brown and Son has a very poor opinion of the book now under his consideration."

And again, quite as forcible is a little anecdote with which he begins an unfinished paper on "Genius." The story is, I now believe, his own; though, at the time, I fancied it was adopted:

"There was once a king who sat to listen to the sermon of a great preacher. From minute to minute the great words flowed on, consoling, wounding, helping, condemning, dividing the marrow from the bones; and the king wept and smiled.

"And at the end he sent for the preacher, and said, 'Sir, Christ is the only king; yet let me look at the book from which you made your discourse. The written words, though half despoiled of their grace, may perhaps strike an echo in my soul, which rings yet.'

"And for some time the preacher was unwilling, and parleyed with the king; but at the last he drew out a little pale book with faded characters traced in ink; and he opened it at a well-worn page, and held it out before the king.

"And the king looked, and saw nothing except the crabbed printed lines.

"So he said, 'Not your text-book, sir, but the book from which your arguments are rehearsed.'

"'Sire,' said the preacher, 'look but once more upon the book.' And he showed him that four of the words upon the page had a thin line drawn in ink below them. 'That was the writing of my discourse,' he said."

Neither, it must be remembered, was Arthur a first-rate conversationalist. He did not steer a conversation; he could keep the ball going creditably when it was once started; but he never communicated to the circle in which he was that indefinable interest which is so intangible and yet so unmistakable.

The two points that I spoke of that he is always trying to work out in his books are:

(1) the strength of temperament, and the difficulty, almost impossibility, of altering it. "The most we can do is to register change," are the first words of his novel. In this book, the situation of which is not a very unusual one, the hero falls in love with one of two sisters, of rare personal beauty and attractiveness, but no particular intellect. He soon wearies of her, being of that fantastic, weak, discontented spirit which Arthur invariably portrayed in his heroes—drawing it I can not conceive whence—and then falls in love with the other, as he ought to have done all along, being, as she is, fully his

match in intellect, and far above him in heart and strength of character. The wife at the crisis of this other love, is killed in a street accident, and remorse ensues. But the book is a weary one; it bears upon its face the burden of sorrow. "How could this have been otherwise?" is the keynote of the story.

Along with this, and indeed as a development of this central principle, is the tendency to treat and write of "sin" so called, wrong-doing, failure of ideal, as variations of spiritual health, as diseases, the ravages of which it is possible for the skilful hand to palliate, but not to cure; to think of and treat sin as a hideous contagion, which has power for a season, perhaps inherently, to drag souls within its grasp, involve and overwhelm them; and consequently to regard the sinner with the deepest sympathy and pity, but with hardly any anger: in fact, I have known him very seriously offend the company he has been in, I have even heard him stigmatized as of loose principles, from his readiness, even anxiety, to condone a sensual offence in a man of high intellect and brilliant gifts.

"He went wrong," he said very sternly, "through having too much passion; and that we can judge him, proves that we have not enough. Well, we shall both of us have to become different: he to be brought down to the harmonious mean, we to be screwed up to it. It is easy to see which will be the most painful process: as soon as *he* gets an idea of whither he is being led, how thankful he will be for every pang that teaches him restraint, and purifies; while we—we shall suffer blind wrench after wrench, *stung* into feeling at any cost, and not till we painfully overtop the barrier shall we guess whither we are going."

I do not mean from this that he thought lightly of sin—far from it. I have seen him give all the physical signs of shrinking and repulsion, at the mention or sight of it. He loathed it with all the agonized disgust of a high, pure, fastidious nature. Its phenomena were without the lurid interest for him which it often possesses even for the sternest moralist.

This loathing had its physical antitype in his horror of the sight or description of bodily disease. I have seen him several times go off into a dead faint at even the bare description of bodily suffering. I went with him once, at his own request, to a seaman's hospital, where there was a poor fellow who had fallen from a mast and been terribly smashed. His legs had both been amputated, and he lay looking terribly white and emaciated with a cradle over the stumps.

He gave us, with great eagerness, an account of the accident, as people in the lower classes always will. In the middle, Arthur stepped suddenly to the door and went out. I was not aware at the time of this failing of his, and the move was executed with such deliberate directness that I thought he must have forgotten something. When I went out to the open air I found Arthur, deadly pale, sitting on the grassy paving-stones of the little yard. He insisted, as soon as he was restored, in going in to wish good-bye to the man, which he accomplished with great difficulty.

But I have already digressed too far, and must return to the main issue.

I am not aware that he ever attempted any theoretical explanation of the intrusion of sin and disorder into the world. He certainly regarded them as emanating practically, in some way that he did not comprehend, from God.

"I can not for a moment believe that these apparent disorders, physical suffering, and the deeper diseases of the will are the manifestation of some inimical power, and not under God's direct control. I have had so much experience of even the immediate blessing of suffering, that I am content to take the rest on trust. If I thought there was some ghastly enemy at work all the time, I should go mad. The power displayed is so calm, so far-reaching, and so divine, that I should feel that even if some of us were finally emancipated from it by the working of some superior power, the contest would be so long and terrible and the issues so dire, that the limited human mind could not possibly contemplate it, that hope would be practically eliminated by despair."

In the same connection, he wrote a letter to a friend whose wild and wayward life had injured his health, and wrote in the greatest agony of mind:

"Words are such wretched things, my dear friend, in crises like this. I can only beg of you, with all my heart, to resolutely set your face against thinking what might have been. Try to feel, I will not say happy, but stronger in the thought that your punishment is atoning for your past every hour. Throw remorse and fear down, if you can; they are only keeping you from God. Many, too many souls are in a far worse case. Some have more to reproach themselves with. On some it has come with what appears to be fearful injustice. Accept your present condition; brace yourself to bear it. I know how much can be borne. Give your sufferings to God nobly. Your patience is none the less noble because you have brought this on yourself; nay, it makes it even nobler....

"Don't say that many worse sinners go unpunished. How can you tell? How do you know they are not suffering? There are only, I suppose, two men in the world, besides yourself, who know that you are suffering now, and why. God visited me with suffering once; He has brought me through, and I have never ceased to thank Him for it; and He will bring you through, too, dear friend, I know. 'Pro jucundis aptissima quæque dabunt di; carior est illis homo quam sibi.' That thought has left me patient, if not glad, in many a bitter hour.... You are never out of my thoughts."

And this letter leads me naturally to the second great principle that pervaded all his writings—"the education of individuals."

"One is inclined to believe that there is a great deal of hopeless irremediable suffering in the world—suffering of a kind that seems wantonly inflicted, purposeless anguish.... That 'regret must hurt and may not heal' is a terrible thought, which, when we get our first glimpse of human anguish, seems almost sickeningly true. But I have seen a great deal lately of such suffering, and it amazes me to discover how *extraordinarily* rare it is to find the victim taking this view of his case. Either it seems to be a due reward for past action—that 'invita religio' which wells up in the blackest heart, or the sufferer gains a kind of onlook into sweet plains beyond, into which the troubled passage is taking him, and which can only thus be reached....

"Of animal suffering, unconscious tortures, it is harder to speak—of the innocent, for so they are, victims of lust and brutality in Babylon here, whose sense of suffering is almost gone, and is succeeded by nothing but the desire for rest; all this seems so meaningless, so futile....

"It is one of the problems I take up and let drop—take up and let drop a thousand times; but all sacrifice seems essentially good, and I do not throw the enigma aside in anger; I will wait for it to be explained to me.

"Ah, death, death, if we are enlightened enough by that time, what a storehouse of secrets, dear secrets you will have to tell us! I thrill all through, in moments like these, to think of it."

"Of course," he said to me once, "there are times when we can only wait and hope; changing our posture, like a sick man, from time to time, to win a little ease; but when we reach a fresh standpoint, a fresh basis—which, thank God, one does from month to month—we are inclined to say with Albert Dürer, 'It could not be better done.'"

He was very fond of the doctrine of Special Providences.

"Every now and then I have—I suppose it is common—what may be called a run of luck in ordinary things; I get out of scrapes in a way I don't deserve; I find letters I have mislaid; annoyances are mysteriously shunted aside; money flows in; days of extraordinary happiness succeed one another; little events save vast complications of trouble, so that I long to turn round and grasp by the hand or kiss the cheek of the sweet friend who stands at my elbow, suggesting, ordering, providing day and night, smiling on me as I sleep, hovering around me as I work, without a word of praise.

Guardian angels! no fable. God gives you a sudden and particular thought, and while you are independent of circumstances you master them as well."

But such portraiture as the above is apt to get very vague and insipid unless one is able to convey a vivid picture of the man as he walked, and spoke, and lived. The *sic sedebat* in Trinity College (Cambridge) chapel has given more people a thrill at the thought of Bacon than ever gained one from his books. Personality, personal characteristics, how one craves for them! To take a late instance, how far more impressive General Gordon's little cane is, which he twirled in his hand as he stormed redoubts and directed an action, than a thousand pages of rhetoric about his philosophy or his views of life.

He was now, as ever, for strangers meeting him for the first time, an impressive but rather disappointing man. He had shaved his beard, keeping only his usual moustache; his face was very spare, with a pallor that was not unhealthy. His hair, which was dark and lay in masses, he wore generally rather long. He had got into the way, when without his glasses, of half closing his eyes, because, as he said, it did him so little good to keep them open, as it only served to remind him of people's presence without giving him any more definite idea of them. He could not, for instance, unassisted, see the play of features on a face, and, for this reason, in all important interviews he wore his glasses, giving three reasons.

1. Utilitarian—that he could see by his opponent's face what he was driving at, and what effect his own remarks had on him.

2. Impressional—it gave a man an "adventitious consequence."

3. Precautional—"I show emotion quickest by the eye, and so, generally speaking, do most people; some change colour very quick; some reveal it in the mouth; but the sudden dilatation and contraction of the eye, the expression it is capable of, make it on the whole the safest guide.

"I trust the eye on the whole," he said; "guilelessness and an unstained conscience are not really manifested either in feature or deportment, but the eye will almost always tell you true."

His conversation, when he was in form, was, without exactly being very brilliant, very inspiring. He had great freshness of expression, and told very few stories, and those only in illustration, never on their own merits. He was very μνημονικός, or retentive—the first requisite, says Plato, of a philosopher—and was consequently well supplied with quotations and allusions, not slavishly repeated, but worked naturally in. I do not mean that he passed for a good talker by skilful plagiarizing, but I found that the wider my range of reading became the more I appreciated his talk—drawn, as it was, from all kinds of sources, and bringing with it that aroma of a far-reaching mind, the *fascination* that culture can bestow, the feeling that, after all, everything is interesting, and that no knowledge is unworthy of the attention of the philosopher.

He hardly ever discussed current politics, though he would argue on political principles with the greatest keenness: neither had he accurate historical knowledge, or antiquarian; but he enjoyed listening to such talk. For the principles, the poetic aspect, of science he had a devoted interest. In literary matters I seldom heard his equal. Many and many is the book which I have been induced to read solely by hearing him sketch the purport in little sentences of extraordinary felicity. "The birth and fatal effects of Impulse in a prosaic soul," was a sketch he gave of a celebrated novel. On one subject he was always dumb—Economics. "It is the one subject on which I have never hazarded a remark successfully," he said to me once. "I can never appreciate the value of an economic statement; I hardly know whether it is interesting."

As he never talked for talking's sake, he was always ready to give his whole attention to the person he was talking to, or none at all; and consequently he never had a middle reputation—some praising his courtesy, as an old lady with whose querulous complaints about ingratitude and rheumatism he had borne and sympathized; others, his abrupt atrocious manner—"Turned his back on me with a scowl, and didn't say another word," as a sporting fast married lady said to me, who had attempted to tell him an improper story. "I didn't mean to offend him; young men generally like it. I hate a young man to be a prude and a Puritan. Why, he isn't even going into the church, I understand!"

One of his colleagues in the school where he was a master, told me that Arthur had once given him a most delicate and pointed rebuke on the practice into which he had fallen, of appealing to a boy's home feelings before the class.

"Some things ought to be said to people when they are alone; besides, we must not *seethe the kid in his mother's milk.*"

The same man told me that he heard him give a little address to the boys in his class, on the two main virtues of a schoolboy—purity and honesty— on the words, "And they said, Lord, behold, here are two swords; and he said unto them, It is enough."

Those are the only two anecdotes I have heard of his professional life, both illustrating that extraordinary gift of apt quotation and seeing unexpected connections, which, to my mind, is as adequate an external symbol of genius as can be found, though sometimes illusory.

He took the greatest delight in the society of children. He writes—

"What wonderful lines those are of Tennyson's"—they had just come out,—"'Who pleased her with a babbling heedlessness Which often lured her from herself!' There is nothing more absolutely refreshing when one is overdone or anxious, or oppressed by the vague anxieties of the world, than the conversation and the society of children, the unconscious ignoring of all grave possibilities, yet often accompanied by that curious tact which divines that all is not well with their older friend, and prompts them to employ all their resources to beguile it. I have been thanked by worldly mothers, in country houses, with something like a touch of nature, for being so good to their boys—'I am so afraid they must have been troublesome to you,'—when they have not only saved me from vapid hard gabble and slanderous gossip, but let in a little breath of paradise as well. I often accept an invitation with reference to the children I shall see. 'To meet Lord and Lady D——, and Mrs. G——, such an amusing woman—tells *such* stories, they make you *scream!*' the invitation runs; and I accept it, to see Johnny and Charlie, to play at Red Indians in the wilderness, and to dig up the tin box of date-stones and cartridge-cases that we buried in the bed of the stream."

If I seem to have given rather a priggish picture of Arthur, it is a totally erroneous one. He was far too casual and too retiring to be that; he had no appearance of self-importance, though an invincible reserve of self-respect. The prig wears chain armor outside, and runs at you with his lance when he catches a glimpse of you. Arthur wore his chain armor under his shirt, and it was not till you closed with him that you felt how sharp his dagger was.

I give a perfectly disinterested sketch of him, which a lady, who met him several times, wrote out at my request. It is hard for me to help speaking from inside knowledge.

"Dear Mr. Carr,

"You ask me to give you my impression of Mr. Hamilton, in writing. What your motive is I can't conceive, as he was not a person I took much interest in, though I know that some people do. Unless, perhaps, you mean to put him into a book.

"I met him at a country house in Shropshire. He came down rather late for breakfast, and when he was asked how he was, he quoted something about 'being apt to be rather fatigued with his night's rest.' I remember it very clearly, because it struck me as being so pointless at the time. He went out shooting most of the day, and I think, as far as I can remember, he was a good shot. He smoked a fearful amount, 'all the time,' in fact; they were always attacking him for that. When he came in he used to have some tea in the nursery. We found that out the last day—the children were sent for, and

Mr. Hamilton came down with them, looking rather sheepish, and saying that he had tried sitting on at one side of the table, with the nursery maid at the other, after the children had gone, but that it didn't do. I remember we were very much amused at the idea; the picture was such a ridiculous one.

"The children certainly seemed to like him extraordinarily—they would talk to no one else: and I can't think why, because children are so impressionable, and he had quite the gravest face I ever saw—almost forbidding. However, so it was.

"He used to disappear to his room, to read and write, before dinner. At dinner he was often very good fun. I have heard him tell some very funny stories, not very racy perhaps, but amusing; and these, coming from that grave face, were very ridiculous. He always made friends with the younger ladies. He never seemed to flirt, and yet he used to say things to them in public that even I felt inclined to pull him up for. And then he used to ask them to go out walks with him, and, what's more, he went out with certainly two, alone; and you know that is rather a marked thing.

"He looked about forty, but he always gravitated toward the young people; made great friends with boys, and in a curious way, too. Generally, if men make friends with schoolboys in a country house it is at the loss of their dignity—they run the risk of having to swallow all sorts of practical jokes, such as getting water thrown on their head and salt put into their tea; but he never compromised himself, and they always behaved to him with respect, but were quite impatient if he wouldn't come with them everywhere. I overheard him talking to a boy once, and I didn't so much wonder; he spoke in such an affectionate way, and boys like to feel that grown-up people take the trouble to like them.

"He was very friendly with the governess, and would try to include her in the conversation. I can't say he succeeded, for we were down on that. I don't myself consider it good form to encourage your governess to have opinions.

"Everybody was always very deferential to him. He always made a sensation if he came into the room. No one could help looking at him. He wasn't one of those tame sneaking creatures that are to be met in country houses, of whom no one takes the least notice; he was much more inclined to take no notice of any one else; but it was impossible to forget he was in the room. And the servants were invariably respectful to him, quite as if he was a real swell; and yet he didn't dress well and hadn't a servant of his own. He was just the sort of man you would have thought flunkeys would have despised.

"But I have let my pen run on to an unconscionable length. It reminds me of the remark with which he dismissed the subject of poor old Sir Charles W— — who was staying there. We had been discussing him, and asked Mr. Hamilton what he thought of him. 'A talking jackass,' was his only reply, in his most chilling tones.

"I fear I am open to the same imputation.

"Very truly yours,
"Laura F— —.

"I should like to know what you want this for; however, happily, I have put it in a form you can't make much use of."

I was much amused at the way in which he treated gossip about himself.

I told him some stories about him that I had picked up. They related to a certain absent-mindedness which he was supposed to possess.

"I am afraid they are not true," he said first. "I should welcome any hint of absence of mind in myself as a sign that the abstract could exclude the concrete, which is unfortunately not the case with me." Then, in a moment, he said, "People have no business to tell such stories. I should not mind their not being true, if they were only characteristic."

"By which you mean," said a gentleman who was sitting next him, "that you don't care about veracity, only you can't stand dullness."

"Not at all," said Arthur, quickly. "Veracity is not the question in gossip at all. It is all hearsay. You have not to judge of the actual truth of a scandalous story, but you have to judge of the probable truth of it, and if it is obviously uncharacteristic it is wrong to repeat it. It becomes scandal then, and not till then."

When he was living in London, which was, for the time being, his home, he lived a regular life, combining more reading with a sociable life than many people would have thought possible. He had two rooms in a house in Russell Square. He breakfasted at half-past nine and read till four, when he went down to his club and talked, or strolled in the park. He made hardly any engagements, except for the evening; and admitted hardly anyone, except two or three friends, to see him at his rooms, and then only after one o'clock, before which hour he was absolutely invisible. He was so dreadfully angry with his landlady for showing a gentleman in once in the middle of the morning, that she literally refused ever to do it again. "He's a good regular lodger, sir, and doesn't think of money, but he said to me, 'Mrs. Laing, I *don't choose to be disturbed* before one. If I find my orders disregarded again, I shall leave the house *that day*.' I daren't do it, sir. You wouldn't like to deprive me of my lodger, I know, sir." The last pathetic plea could not be gainsaid, so Arthur had his way.

Four evenings he devoted to going out, and the other three dining quietly at home and reading. By the time he left London his reading, always wide, had become prodigious. His own library was good, and he had a ticket for the British Museum Reading-room and belonged to two circulating libraries. He made a point of reading new books (1) if he was strongly recommended them by specialists; (2) if they reached a second edition within a month; (3) if they were republished after a period of neglect—this he held to be the best test of a book.

It was characteristic of his natural indolence that he chose the very easiest method of reading—that is to say, he always read, if he could, *in a* translation, or if the style of the original was the object, *with* one. This, like his posture, nearly recumbent, was deliberately adopted. "I find," he said, "that the *reflective* part of my brain works best when I have as little either bodily or *purely* intellectual to distract me as possible. And it is the reflective part," he says, "that I always preferred to cultivate, and that latterly I have devoted my whole attention to. It is through the reflective part that one gets the highest influence over people. Training the reflective function is the training of character, while the training of the purely physical side often, and the training of the intellectual side not uncommonly, have a distinctly deteriorative effect.

"By the reflective part, I mean all that deals with the *connection* of things, the discovery of principles, the laws that regulate emotion and influence, the motives of human nature, the basis of existence, the solution of the problem of life and being—that vast class of subjects which lie just below, and animate concrete facts, and which are the only things worthy of the devotion of a philosopher, though no knowledge is unworthy of his *attention*.

"I am not quite clear what position I intend to take up in the world at large. This only is certain, that if I am going to teach, and I have a vague sense that I am destined for that, it is necessary first to know something, to be *sure* of something."

All his days were alike, except that on Sunday he used to frequent city churches in the afternoon, or go to Westminster Abbey and St. Paul's. His father was a friend of a canon at the former place, and Arthur was generally certain of a stall; and I used often to see his tall form there, with his eyes "indwelling wistfully," "reputans secum," as Virgil says, lost in speculations and wonders, and a whole host of melancholy broodings over life and death to which he rarely gave voice, but which formed a perpetual background to his thoughts. He varied this by visits to his father in Hampshire, and occasional trips to the country, not unfrequently alone, the object and occupation of which he never told me, except to say once that he had explored, he thought, every considerable "solitude" in England.

There is one thing that I must not forget to mention—his dreams. He never slept, he told me, without innumerable dreams, and he not unfrequently told me of them. They always struck me as curiously vivid. I subjoin the following from one of his diaries. They are often given at full length. This is one of the most interesting I can find.

"*January* 8.—Slept badly; toward morning dreamed that I was walking with two or three friends, and accompanied by a tall man whom I did not know, wrapped in a cloak, through a very dark wood. I seemed to be in a very heavy mood. We came upon a building brightly lighted, and, entering, found a hall with many people dining. There was much wine and talk, and a great deal of laughing and merriment. We appeared to be invisible.

"I began to moralize aloud. I said, 'Yes, and this is the way in which lives pass: a little laughter and a few jests and a song or two; forgetful, all the time, that the lights must be extinguished and the wine spilled, and that night laps them round,'—catching, as I said this, a glimpse of the dark trees swaying outside.

"But the man in the cloak took me up. 'This shows,' he said, 'how superficial your view is—how little you look below the surface of things. This laughter and light talk are but the signs and symbols of qualities of which your bitter character knows nothing—goodfellowship, kindliness, brave hopefulness, and many things beside.'

"Then he turned to me impressively, and said, 'What you want is *deepening*.'

"I woke with the word ringing in my ears."

Besides this, there was a curious little peculiarity in him that I have never heard of in anyone else: a capacity for seeing little waking visions with strange distinctness.

His description of this is as follows:

"I have the power, or rather something in me is able (for I can not resist it), of suddenly producing a picture on the retina, of such vividness as to blot out everything around me. I have it generally when I am a little tired with exercise or brain-work or people: it is prefaced by seeing a bright blue spot, which moves, or rather rushes, across my field of vision, and is immediately succeeded by the picture.

"A crumbling sandstone temple, among fields of blue flowers—an obelisk carved with figures, in a wood—a gray indistinct marsh, with mist rising from it, and by the edge a white bird, egret or something similar, of dazzling whiteness—a green lane, with cows in it. I could go on for ever enumerating them. They pass in a fraction of a second, three or four succeeding one another. My eyes are not shut, nor do I look different. I have always seen them. I was alarmed about them once, and went to a doctor; but he said he could not explain it—it was probably a nervous idiosyncrasy: and I felt all the better for my habit having a name."

One more thing I must mention about him, which I have discovered since his death. I must add *that I never had the least suspicion of it in his life.*

He was the victim during this time of a depression of mind; not constant, but from which he never felt secure. I subjoin a few entries from his diaries.

"Very troubled and gloomy: a strange heart-sinking—a blank misgiving without any adequate cause upon me all day. One can not help feeling during such times—and, alas! they are becoming very familiar to me—that some mysterious warfare may be being fought out somewhere over one's only half-conscious soul: that some strange decision may be pending." And again: "For the last week, my mind—though I have reiterated again and again to myself that it is purely physical—has steadily refused to take any view of life, to have any outlook, except the most dismal. I am a little better to-day—well enough to see the humour of it, though God knows it is black enough while it lasts."

In one letter he wrote to me, I find the following words: it never occurred to me at the time that they were the gradual fruits of his own experience on the subject:

"Physical and mental depression is a most fearful enemy. Other things give you trouble at intervals—toothache, headache, etc., are all spasmodic afflictions, and, moreover, can be much mitigated by circumstances. But with depression it is not so: it poisons any cup—it turns all the cheerful little daily duties of life into miseries, unutterable burdens; death is the only future event which you can contemplate with satisfaction. It admits of no comfort: the whispered suggestion of the mind, 'You will be better soon,' falls on deaf ears. No physical suffering that I have ever felt, and I have not been without my share, is in the least comparable to it; the agony of foreboding remorse and gloom with which it involves past, present, and future—there is nothing like it. It is the valley of the Shadow of Death.

"But when one first realizes how purely physical it is, it is an era. I endured it for two years first: now I am prepared. I may even say that though all sense of enjoyment dies under it, my friends, the company I am in, generally suspect nothing."

This was literally the case. I knew his spirits were never very high; but he seemed to me to maintain, what is far more valuable, a genial equable flow of cheerfulness, such as one would give much to possess.

Among his occasional diversions at this time, I must place visiting some of the worst houses in one of the worst quarters in London.

It was not then a fashionable habit, and he never spoke of it or made capital out of his experience; but he went to have an acquaintance that should be *teres et rotundus* with all phases of life. He never attempted to relieve misery by indiscriminate charity; his principles were strongly against it.

"I don't profess to understand the economical condemnation of indiscriminate charity. I don't see why one set of people should not spend in necessaries what another set would only spend in luxuries.

"But I do understand this: that it does infinite harm, by accustoming the poor to think that all the help they will get from the upper classes till they rise up themselves and lay hands upon it, will be indiscriminate half-sovereigns. The clergy are beginning to disabuse them of this idea. It is a fact which does appeal to them when they see a man that they recognize belongs by right to the 'high life' and could drive in his carriage, or at any rate in somebody else's, and have meat four times a day—when they see such a man coming and staying among them, certainly not for pleasure or money, or even, for a long time, at least, love, it impresses them far more than the Non-conformists or Revivalists who attempt the same kind of thing.

"And that's the sort of help I want them to look for—intelligent sympathy and interest in them. To most of them no amount of relief or education could do any good now; it would only produce a rank foliage of vice, which is slightly restrained by hard labour and hard food. Sensualism is a taint in their blood now.

"They want elevating and refining in some way, and you can only do it with brutes through their affections."

His manner with poor people was very good—direct, asking straightforward questions and not making his opinions palatable, and yet behaving to them with perfect courtesy, as to equals.

We were staying in a house together in the country once, and heard that a certain farmer was in trouble of some kind—we were not exactly told what.

Arthur had struck up a friendship with this man on a previous visit, and so he determined to go over and see him. He asked me to ride with him, and I agreed. I will describe the episode precisely as I can remember it:

We rode along, talking of various things, over the fresh Sussex downs, and at last turned into a lane, overhung on both sides with twisted tree-roots of fantastic shape, writhing and sprawling out of the crumbling bank of yellow sand. Presently we came to a gap in the bank, and found we were close to the farm. It lay down to the right, in a little hollow, and was approached by a short drive inclosed by stone walls overgrown by stonecrop and pennywort, and fringed with daffodils and snap-dragons: to the left, the wall was overtopped by the elders of a copse; to the right, it formed one side of a fruit garden.

The drive ended in a flagged yard, upon which our horse's hoofs made a sudden clatter, scaring a dozen ducks into pools and other coigns of vantage, and rousing the house-dog, who, with ringing chain and surly grumbles, came out blinking, to indulge in several painful barks, waiting, as dogs will, with eyes shut and nose strained in the air, for the effect of each bark, and consciously enjoying the tuneful echo. A stern-featured, middle-aged woman came out quickly, almost as if annoyed at the interruption, but on seeing who it was she dropped a quick courtsey, and spoke sharply to the dog.

Arthur went forward, holding out his hand.

"We were so sorry to hear at the house," he said, "that there was trouble here. I did not learn quite clearly what it was, but I thought I would ride over to see if there was anything I could do."

Arthur knew quite enough of the poor to be sure that it was always best to plunge straight into the subject in hand, be it never so grim or painful. Life has no veneering for them; they look hard realities in the face and meet them as they can. They are the true philosophers, and their straightforwardness about grief and disease is not callousness; it is directness, and generally means as much, if not more, feeling than the hysterical wailings of more cultivated emotion, more organized nerves.

"Yes, sir," she said to me, with that strange dignity of language that trouble gives to the poor, just raising her apron to her eyes, "it's my master, sir—Mr. Keighley, sir. The doctor has given him up, and he's only waiting to die. It don't give him much pain, his complaint; and it leaves his head terrible clear. But he's fearful afraid to die, sir; and that's where it is.

"Not that he's not lived a good life; been to church and paid his rent and tithe reg'lar, been sober and industrious and good to his people; but I think, sir," she said, "that there's one kind of trembling and fearfulness that we can't get over: he keeps saying that he's afraid to meet his God. He won't say as he's got anything on his mind; and, truthfully, I don't think he has. But he can't go easy, sir; and I think a sight of your face, if I may make so bold, would do him, maybe, a deal of good."

"I shall be very glad to see him, if he cares to see me," said Arthur. "Has Mr. Spencer" (the clergyman) "been here?"

"Yes, sir," said the woman; "but he don't seem to do George no good. He's prayed with him—the Church prayers out of his blue prayer-book; but, after that, all he could say was, 'you must prepare to meet your God; are you at peace with Him? Remember the judgment;' when I can't help thinking that God would be much more pleased if George could forget it. He can't like to see us crawling to meet Him, and cryin' for fear, like as Watch does if his master has beat him for stealin'. But I dare not say so to him, sir—we never know, and I have no right to set myself up over the parson's head."

I confess that I felt frightfully helpless as we followed her into the house. There was a bright fire burning; a table spread in a troubled untidy manner, with some unfinished food, hardly tasted, upon it.

She said apologetically, "You see, sir, it's hard work to keep things in order, with George lying ill like this. I have to be always with him."

"Of course," said Arthur, gently. "I know how hard it is to keep up heart at all; still it is worth trying: we often do better than we expect."

His sweet voice and sympathetic face made the poor woman almost break down; she pushed hastily on, and, saying something incoherently about leading the way, ushered us through a kitchen and up a short flight of stairs. I would have given a great deal to have been allowed to stay behind. But Arthur walked simply on behind the woman.

"I won't tell him you're here," she said; "he'd say he wasn't fit to see you. But it won't harm him; maybe it'll even cheer him up a bit." She pushed the door open just above; I could distinguish the sound of hard breathing, with every now and then a kind of catch in the breath, and a moan; then we found ourselves inside the room.

The sick man was lying propped up on pillows, with a curious wistful and troubled look on his face, which altered very quickly as we came in. Much of his suffering was nervous, so-called; and a distraction, any new impression which diverted his mind, was very helpful to him.

"George," said the woman, "here is Mr. Hamilton and his friend come over from the Squire's to see you."

He gave a grateful murmur, and pointed to a chair.

"I am so sorry," said Arthur, simply, "to see you in such suffering, Mr. Keighley. We heard you were in trouble, so we thought we would ride over and see if we could do anything for you."

"Thank you, sir, kindly," said the sick man, feebly. "But I'm past doin' anything for now. Doctor's giv'n me up; he gives me a week. But thank you all the same."

He closed his eyes for a moment; and then, looking round quickly, fingering the counterpane, he said, "Ah, sir, this isn't a place for you to be in; but I take it very kindly of you. Ah! Ah! It seems as if it might have been made a bit easier, might dyin'. It's hard work—it's terrible hard. It's bad enough by itself, having to go out into the dark—and all alone; but it's full of worse terrors than even that. The air's full of them. When I am lyin' here still, with my eyes shut, prayin' for it all to be over, I seem to hear them buzzin' and whisperin' in the air. Then it comes, all on a sudden, on me—here"—putting his hand to his heart. "It makes me sick and trembling—with fear and horror—I can't bear it. It's comin' now. Ah! Ah! Ah!"

I remember feeling inexpressibly shocked and horrified. I was not used to such scenes. The room seemed to swim; I could hardly stand or see. To settle myself, I spoke to the woman about wines and medicines; but I seemed to hear my own voice hollow and from a distance, and started at the sound of it.

But Arthur knelt simply down by the bedside and said, "I think it will make it easier if you can only fix your thoughts on one thing. I know the effort is hard; but think that there's a loving hand waiting to take yours; there's One that loves you, better than you have ever loved anyone yourself, waiting the other side of the darkness. Oh, only think of that, and it will not be hard! Dear friend," he said—"for I may call you that—we have all of us the same passage before us, but we have all the same hope: and He hears the words you speak to Him. He has been here, He is here now, to listen to your very thoughts. He has seen your trouble, and wished He could help you—why He can not I am not able to tell you; but it will all be well.

"Let me say one prayer with you." And he began in his low quiet voice. The woman knelt down beside him, shaken with sobbing. Till, at the words "Suffer us not, for any pains of death, to fall from thee," poor George put out his old withered hand and took Arthur's, and smiled through his pain— "the first time he ever smiled since his illness began," his wife told us after his death, "and he smiled many times after that."

He did not speak to us again; the effort had been too great. The woman accompanied us down-stairs, showing, in her troubled officious hurry to anticipate Arthur's wishes, and the way in which she hung about the gate as we rode out, what it had been to her.

We rode home almost in silence. Arthur, as we got near to the lodge, turned to me, and said, half apologetically, "We must speak to simple people in the language that they can understand. Fortunately, there is one language we can all understand."

CHAPTER IX

It was a hot summer, and Arthur a little overtasked his strength. London, and a London season, is far more tiring than far greater physical exertions in pure air and with rational hours. He complained of feeling liable to faintness after standing about in hot rooms. It did not cause him, however, any serious alarm, till one evening he fainted after a dinner-party at which I was present, and we had some difficulty in bringing him round.

After this, for several days he spoke of an invincible languor which held him throughout the day, which he could not get rid of; and he was altogether so unlike his usual self, and so prostrate, that at last, with the greatest difficulty, I prevailed on him to see a doctor—a thing he particularly disliked.

He made an appointment with a celebrated physician in Wimpole Street. As he was far from well on the morning he was to go there, I insisted on accompanying him.

He was in very cheerful spirits, and was eagerly discussing a book which had just been published; he could not make up his mind whether it had been written by a man or a woman. He said that there was always one character in a book, not always the hero or heroine, through whose eyes the writer seemed to look, whose mental analysis seemed to have the ring not of description, but confession, and this would be found to be, he maintained, of the sex of the writer. In the particular case under discussion, where the hero was a man, he professed to discover the "spy," as he called this character, in a woman.

In the middle of the discussion we drew up at Dr. Hall's door, and were immediately shown into one of those rooms with a professional and suspicious calm about it. "'Five minutes before the drop falls,' it seems to say; 'make your mind quite easy; feel chatty,'" said Arthur.

He looked curiously about him, and commented humorously on the selection of literature, till a patient was ushered out, and we were called in.

Dr. Hall was not the least what one is inclined to think a celebrated doctor should be. Arthur had been describing his ideal to me—"tall and pale; stoops slightly, but very distinguished-looking, with piercing grey eyes, a kindly reassuring manner, and grey whiskers cut straight."

Dr. Hall was a small sallow man, with rather an agitated fussy manner, and eyes that never seemed to be looking at you. He was neat, almost dapper, in his dress, and was rather like the butler in a small establishment.

He put one or two questions to Arthur; stethoscoped him, hovering all about restlessly; suddenly caught up his left hand and pushed aside the first finger; "Ah, cigarette-smoker—we must put a stop to that at once, if you please. What is your usual allowance?"

"It varies," said Arthur, "but I fear it is never less than twenty."

"Four, after this date," said Dr. Hall.

"Just come into my other room a moment," he said presently, and led the way.

Arthur followed, giving me a cheerful wink. They remained about ten minutes, during which time I speculated, and read a little book about Epping Forest, which was on the table; looked out of the window, and felt rather ill myself.

At last, the tall door creaked, and Arthur came out, followed by the doctor.

"I hope you will see, sir," he said to me, "that Mr. Hamilton is particular in following my directions, if you have any influence with him."

"I am afraid I haven't got the temperament of a patient," said Arthur, smiling. "But I am very much obliged to you. Good morning."

"What did he say to you?" I said, as soon as we were in our cab again.

"Oh, he spoke to me like a father," said Arthur: "gave me a lot of wretched directions which I know I shan't attend to. But we have wasted much too much time medically already this morning." And he changed the subject to the discussion which we had been carrying on before.

A few days after this I went to see him, and found him much better.

"What do you think?" he said: "I am going to undertake the charge of a human being. Do you remember our conversation about adopting children, and the educational experiments we meant to try? I shall have the chance now."

On my inquiring what had happened, he told me his experience at Teheran, related in a former chapter; and said that, on reflection, he had thought well to accept the commission, adding that he had been surprised to find waiting for him, when he had returned home at a late hour a few nights before his visit to Dr. Hall, a tall foreign gentleman, who had introduced himself as a friend of Mr. Bruce's (so the recluse chose to call himself), and as the bearer of a message from him, the purport of which was to ask whether he would accept Mr. Bruce's commission.

"I am authorized to state," the stranger added, "in the event of your acquiescing, that the method of procedure will be left entirely to yourself; that no question will be asked or conditions made; the boy will be sent to London or to any other address you may appoint; that £400 a year, quarterly, will be placed to your credit at the Westminster Bank for all necessary expenses; and that a draft in your name, for any further sum that you may think requisite, will be honoured.

"If you would forward your answer to Morley's Hotel, to the address on my card, any time within the next week, I shall be grateful. My instructions are not to press for an immediate answer." And the gentleman bowed himself out.

He showed me a short letter which he had written accepting the charge; and, shortly after, I rose to go. But he detained me rather pointedly; and after a short time, in which he appeared to be considering something, he begged me to sit down again, and consider whether I would listen to a short statement of facts on which he wanted my advice. "They are," he said, "I fear, a little painful, and therefore I do not press it; but I should be sincerely obliged to you."

He then said, "I did not at the time tell you, my dear Chris, what Doctor Hall said to me the other day, because I thought it better to tell no one; but the events of the last week have caused me to change my mind. I feel that I must be perfectly open.

"The fact was, that he warned me that I showed unequivocal symptoms of a dangerous heart disease. He could not answer for anything, he said. I had seen that something was wrong from his expression, so I insisted on knowing everything."

I can hardly describe my sensations at this announcement—I felt the room swim and shake; and yet it was made in such a deliberate matter-of-fact tone, that it flashed across me for an instant that Arthur was joking, and together with it came a curiously dismal sense of unreality, that is well known to all those who have passed through any great strain or emotional crisis, as if, suddenly, the soul had fallen out of everything, and they were nothing but lifeless empty husks, hollow and phantasmal.

"But," I gasped, "you never said anything of this at the time: you—you behaved just as usual."

"I certainly tried to," he said. "And curiously enough, I did not either realize or fear the news at the time; it left my feelings almost blank. I won't deny that it has caused me some painful thought since.... He gave me a few simple directions: I was to avoid bracing climates, hard physical work, or, indeed, mental effort—anything exhausting; to keep regular hours, avoid hot rooms and society and smoking; but that I might do, in moderation, anything that interested me, write or read; and, above all things, I was to avoid agitation.

"I think I intend to put his ideas into practice; not much with the idea of saving my life, for I don't feel particularly anxious about that, but because I think that, on the whole, it is the most sensible kind of life to lead. And the fact that I had already accepted the charge of this boy has finally decided me; it was too late to draw back. I shall settle in some quiet place, and try and educate him for the University. I don't at all expect to be dull; and it evidently wouldn't do to thrust him straight into English life yet—he wants Anglicizing gradually. I hope he will be an average Englishman by the time he gets to Cambridge."

Arthur heard the next day, from Mr. Bruce's agent, that the boy would arrive in the course of a month, so he determined to try and have things ready by then for their retirement.

We went energetically to house agents, and the result was that we were at last blessed by success.

Cornwall was the county that we selected; its warm indolent climate seemed to answer our requirements best, and Arthur would not leave England.

Close to Truro there is a little village called St. Uny Trevise. You have to leave the high-road to get to it. Its grey church tower is a conspicuous landmark for several miles round, standing out above a small wood of wind-swept oaks, on the top of a long broad-backed down, lately converted into farm-land, and ploughed up. About half a mile from this, going by strangely winding deep lanes, you reach the bottom of a wooded dell, very lonely and quiet, with a stream running at the bottom, that spreads out into marshes and rush-beds, with here and there a broad brown pool. Crossing the little ford, for there is only a rude bridge for foot-passengers, and ascending the opposite hill, you find yourself at last, after going up the steep overhung road, at the gate of a somewhat larger house than usual in those desolations.

The gate-posts are stone, with granite balls at the top, and there is a short drive, which brings you to a square mottled front of brown stone, with two large projections, or small wings, on each side.

This is a small manor, known as Tredennis, anciently belonging to the Templeton family, whose pictures ornament the hall. It had been used latterly merely as a farmhouse; but a local solicitor, desiring that a somewhat more profitable arrangement might be made respecting it, had the manor put up at the extremely moderate rent of £60, and banished the farmer to an adjoining tenement.

There was a terraced garden, very rich in flowers in the summer. It faced south and west, commanding a view of a winding valley, very peaceful and still, a great part of which was overgrown with stunted oak copses, or divided into large sloping fields. At the end, the water of a tidal creek—Tressillian water—caught the eye. The only sounds that ever penetrated to the ear were the cries of birds, or the sound of sheep-bells, or the lowing of cows, with an occasional halloo from the farm, children calling among the copses, or the shrill whistle from over the hills, telling of the train, that, burrowing among the downs, tied one to the noisier world.

Truro has been much opened up since then. It has a bishop, and the rudiments of a cathedral. It has burst into a local and spasmodic life. But when I knew it through Arthur, it was the sleepiest and laziest town alive, with the water rippling through the streets. Old-world farmers, with their strange nasal dialect, used to haunt the streets on market day, like the day on which we first drove through it on our way to Tredennis. Arthur was well and serene. He took the keenest delight in the fragrance of retirement that hung about the place: people to whose minds and ears modern ideas, modern weariness, had never penetrated; who lived a serious indolent life, their one diversion the sermon and the prayer-meeting, their one dislike "London ways."

We reached the house in the evening, losing our way more than once in our endeavour to discover it. Two sitting-rooms were furnished, both large airy rooms looking upon the garden, and a bedroom and dressing-room up-stairs, which Arthur and his charge were to occupy. The housekeeper and her handmaiden, who were to be his servants, were already installed, and had arranged in a certain fashion the new furniture that Arthur had sent down, jostling with the old, and his books. As we sat, the first evening, with our cigarettes, in the dusk, watching the green sky over the quiet hills, a wonderful sensation of repose seemed to pass into one from the place. "I feel as if I might be very happy here," said Arthur, "if I were allowed; and perhaps work out my old idea a little more about the meaning of external things."

I was to return to London in a day or two, to see about any commission that might have been neglected, and to bring down the boy, who was now daily expected.

In my absence I received the following letter from Arthur. The serene mood had had its reaction.

"I have told you, I think, of the depressing effect that a new place has on me till I get habituated to it. There is a constant sense of unrest, just as there is about a new person, that racks the nerves.

"I have been very anxious and 'heavy' to-day, as the Psalms have it: dispirited about the future and the present, and remorseful about the past. You don't mind my speaking freely, do you? I feel so weak and womanish, I must tell some one. I have no one to lean on here.

"I can't see what to make of my life, or, rather, what can possibly be made of it. I have taken hitherto all the rebuffs I have had—and they have not been few—as painful steps in an education which was to fit me for something. I was having, I hoped, experience which was to enable me to sympathize with human beings fully, when I came to speak to them, to teach them, to lead them, as I have all my life believed I some day should.

"You won't think it conceited if I say this to you, my dear Chris? I don't feel to myself as if I was like other people. I have met several people better and on a higher level than myself, but no one on quite the same level—no one, to put it shortly, quite so *sure* as I am.

"Does that explain itself? I mean that I have for many years been conscious of a kind of inward law that I dare not disobey, and which has constrained me into obedience—once unwilling, now willing, and even enthusiastic. In others, it has always seemed to me that there is strife and διψυχία—one great factor pulling one way and one another; but it has never been so with me—there has never been a serious strain. I have always known what I meant, and have generally done it; and little by little, as I have lived, comparing this inner presence with what I can see of moral laws, of Divine government, I have come to observe that the two are almost identical, though there are certain variations which I have not yet accounted for.

"Mind, this has been in my case a *negative* influence; it has never urged a course upon me; it has always withheld me. Even in a dilemma of any kind, it never has said, 'Do this;' it is always, 'Avoid that.' So that I have had to take my line, as I have done in practical things, though never in opposition to its warnings.

"I had always thought that I was being educated to the point of describing this subjective law to others, and helping them to some such position. I have always felt that I had a message to deliver, though the manner and method of delivering it I felt I had to discover.

"And so I was led from point to point. I was educated without any special domestic attachments. I was shown that I was not to believe in my friends. And then, at Cambridge, it came upon me that this was what was meant—that I was not to devote myself to mean, selfish objects; that I was not even to be solaced by individual love: but that I was to speak to the world the way of inward happiness by the simplification of the complex issues, the human intricacies, which have gathered round and obscured the whole problem.

"Then I gradually gave up, or thought I was giving up, human ambitions. I took a course which I saw was not to end in human fame, or wealth, or happiness of the ordinary kinds; and that I might test my capacities a little more and learn myself, and also familiarize myself with more aspects of the great question which I was going to face, I travelled among the cities of men and the solitudes of the earth.

"And at last I thought I had found the way; but I will not tell you what it was, for I now see that I was mistaken. I thought I saw that my duty was to come back and speak the first words to the society in which most naturally I moved; and I came to London, as you know. And then I began to write; but I failed there. I was not disheartened, for I felt that I was being led, and that that was not the way. And once I thought that I was to be pointed out the path by the love of a daring woman; but that went from me too, as you know, and so I waited to be shown how to speak.

"But it is not to be; for while I waited, this has fallen upon me; and this is more than I can bear. It is terrible enough, as a human being, to look Death in the face, and question of the blind eye what are the secrets he knows; but I have passed through that before, and I can truly say I do not dread that now. It is rather with an intense and reverent curiosity that I look forward to death, as the messenger that will tell me that my work here is over, and I am to learn God's ways elsewhere. No, it is not that; but it is the utter aimlessness and failure of my life. I have not attracted men's praise—I did not hope to do that. I have not even attracted their attention. I have not communicated the least grain of what I feel I *know*.

"Far from looking upon me as a man who at least sees clearer than others, as having a truth of price which they might be glad to learn, they look upon me as a man who has failed even to live life upon their basis, classing me with those utter failures who fail in life because they have no sense of proportion, because they can not comprehend the complex issues among which they have to fight.

"And now I am laid aside, a useless weapon; I am not even physically capable of writing, even if the world would hear me; and I am forced back upon myself, upon a feeble life, necessarily self-centered, to nurse and coddle myself as though I was a poor failing dotard, with one avenue alone—and how precarious!—through which I may perhaps speak my little message to the world—the education of a child to carry on my torch.

"I have written to you my whole mind, not because I want you to reassure me—no, that is impossible; but because I am weak and miserable. I must unburden myself to some one—must confess that I have indeed broken down.

"And, further, what is the Death, into whose antechamber I have already passed? Is it indeed true that, as I have so passionately denied, I have fallen into the grasp of a power which is waging an equal war with truth and light and goodness? Shall I be sacrificed to the struggle, without having made the world a whit better, or richer, or stronger, with the only memory of me a quiet life with few follies and fewer deeds of power, to be laid away in the dark?

"And yet I have a lingering hope that this is a leading too; that I shall somehow emerge. My dear Chris, come and see me again as soon as you can. You will be even more welcome if you bring my boy, Edward Bruce, as I understand we are to call him—*attamen ipse veni.*

"I am your affectionate friend,
"Arthur Hamilton.

"Flora"—his collie, of whom he was very fond—"is sitting watching me with such liquid eyes that I must go and take her out. We have not walked as far as the creek yet; the first effect of valetudinarian habits is, I find, to make one feel really ill."

On the 4th of August, Tuesday, at 11.15, a card was brought to me, and immediately afterward a tall gentleman appeared, with a boy of about fourteen, whom I knew at once to be Edward Bruce.

The gentleman, after a few polite words of inquiry after Arthur, retired, the boy saying good-bye to him affectionately. He left me his address for a few days, in case I should wish to see him.

Edward Bruce was a boy of extraordinary beauty—there was no denying that. Personal descriptions are always disappointing; but, not to be prolix, he had such eyes, with so much passion and fire in them, that they could only be the inheritance of many generations of love and hate and quick emotions; his eyelids drooped languidly, but when he opened his eyes and looked full at you!—I felt relieved to think I should not have to conduct his education; I could not have denied him anything. His hair was brown and curly, cut short, but of that fineness and glossy aspect that showed that till lately it had been allowed its own way.

The boy had beautiful lips and white regular teeth, with that exquisite complexion that is the result of perfect health and physical condition. He did not speak English very well, but acquired it fast. He always spoke slowly, and with a very pure articulation. His voice was clear, high-pitched, and thrilling—I have no other word for it.

On the following day I took him down to Tredennis. The boy was interested and excited, and asked many questions of a very unsophisticated kind.

"Why do people stare at me so?" he said, turning round from the window of the carriage, in Bristol, where he stood devouring the crowd with hungry eyes. I could not explain to him. He thought it was because of his foreign look, and was much disgusted. "I made them *dress* me like an Englishman," he said, surveying himself. To be English, that was his aim.

I found that his father had inculcated this idea in him thoroughly, and had impressed upon him the dignity of the position. It was, I was told afterward, the one argument that never failed to make him attentive in his lessons.

It was not till he was driving away from Truro into the country that he found leisure to think of his father and brother, and wonder what they would be doing. I had the greatest difficulty in explaining that the hours of the day were different, and that it was early morning there.

"No," he said, "it is impossible; I feel like the evening—Martin can not be feeling like the morning."

He was rather disappointed as we got further and further into the lovely country. "I have lived among trees all my life," he said. "I want to live among people now, in cities, and hear what they say and do what they do. I love them." And he waved his hand to the lights of the town in the valley below us, as a sign of farewell.

At last we drove into the dark gates of Tredennis, and drew up before the house.

Arthur came out to meet us. "Where is Edward?" he said.

The boy sprang out to meet him, and would have kissed him; but Arthur just grasped his hand, retaining it for a moment, and then let him go. The boy kept close to him, examining him attentively, when we got inside the house, with restless, affectionate glances.

"What makes you so pale?" he said.

"Ah!" said Arthur, with a smile, "no one else can tell except ourselves what makes our face so white; but you will be white like this soon," he said: "it is our dark English days, not like your Persian sun."

"Then I shall be glad to be like that," said the boy, "if that is how the English look."

He went off on a tour of exploration about the house, soon discovering his room, with which he was enraptured.

In the garden, later on in the evening, he came to Arthur with a letter in his hand. "This is for you," he said. "I had almost forgotten it. But it is too dark to read it here; I shall fetch you a light." And he brought the lamp out of the house, and stood holding it, as it burnt unwavering in the still night air.

Arthur read it and handed it to me, while the great moths and transparent delicate flies came and blundered against it.

"Edward will give you this letter himself. His hand will touch your hand. It has come about as I anticipated, neither sooner nor later; and I am glad.

"Dear friend, all is not well with you; I heard it in the night. But the passages of the house are often dark, though the hills are full of light; yet the Master's messengers pass to and fro between the high halls bearing lamps; such a messenger I send you.

"You must not be dismayed, either now or later, for all is well. In our mysteries, when the youth first tastes the chalice, he can hardly keep his mind upon the Red Wine of Life, the Blood of the Earth, as he would fain do, for thinking of the cup, and how tremblingly he holds it, and for fear that the crimson juice be spilt; but all the while, though he sees it not, the priest's hand encircles the gold stem.

"Martin, *my* son (for Edward is now yours—mine no longer), is even nearer the end than when I spoke with you; and you too are nearer, far nearer, though you know it not. And even in this little letter, I have spoken words to you which, if you had but light to read them, would make all plain.

"The hour is at hand; the clock has jarred and is silent again, but the gear murmurs on in the darkness, waiting for the silver chiming of the bell.

"I am your friend always,
"B.
"TEHERAN,
"Midsummer."

"A curious document," I said.

"Yes," said Arthur, musingly; "curious too, as literally true." And he pointed to the boy holding the lamp.

"Edward," he said to the boy, "put back that lamp, and come here and speak to me."

The boy went quickly and promptly, delighting in little acts of obedience, as the young do.

When he returned, Arthur said, "Your father says in this letter that you are to be my son for the future. Will you? are you content to change?"

"Yes," said the boy, shyly; but he came and leant against his new father's shoulder where he sat, and, in the pretty demonstrative manner so natural to unsophisticated children, encircled his arm with his hands.

Arthur put his arm round the boy's neck, and stroked his hair caressingly.

"Very well," he said, "then you must always obey me as well as you did just now; and we will make an Englishman of you, and, what is more, a good man."

And we sat in silence, looking down the valley. Every now and then an owl called in his flute-like notes across the thickets, and we heard the cry of the seabirds from the creek; and the soft wind came gently up, rustling the fir over our heads, stirring among the leaves of the tall syringa, and wandering off into the warm dusk.

CHAPTER X

The next day I had to return to London on business, taking leave of the strange household with some regret. Arthur insisted on driving me to the station. He talked very brightly of his experiment, and argued at some length as to how far association could be depended upon as an element in education; and how to distinguish those natures early that were loyal to association and those to whom it would be of no authority.

"I have always divided," he said, "the great influences by which ordinary people are determined to action into two classes; and I have connected them with the two staves that the prophet cut, and named 'Beauty and Bands.'

"Some people are worked upon by Beauty—direct influences of good; they choose a thing because it is fair; they refrain from action because it is unlovely; they take nothing for granted, but have an innate fastidious standard which the ugly and painful offend.

"Others are more amenable to Bands—home traditions, domestic affections: they do not act and refrain from action on a thing's own merits because it is good or bad; but because some one that they have loved would have so acted or so refrained from acting—'My mother would not have done so;' 'Henry would have disliked it.' The idea is fancifully put, but it holds good, I think."

Shortly after my return to London, I got two letters from him of considerable importance. I give them both. The first is apropos of the education of Edward Bruce.

"Tredennis, August 30.

"My Dear Friend,

"I want you to get me the inclosed list of books, which I find are culpably absent from my library. It is a very engrossing prospect, this child's mind: it is a blank parchment, ready for any writing, and apparently anxious for it too.

"'Insight into all seemly and generous acts and affairs,' wrote Milton, as the end of his self-education—something like that I intend, if I am allowed, to give this child. I have the greatest contempt for knowledge and erudition *qua* knowledge and erudition. A man who has laboriously edited the Fathers seems to me only to deserve the respect due to a man who has carried through an arduous task, and one that must have been, to anyone of human feelings and real enthusiasm for ideas, uncongenial at first. Erudition touches the human race very little, but on the 'omne ignotum' principle, men are always ready to admire it, and often to pay it highly, and so there is a constant hum of these busy idlers all about the human hive. The man who works a single practical idea into ordinary people's minds, who adds his voice to the cry, 'It is better to give up than to take: it is nobler to suffer silently than to win praise: better to love than to organize,' whether it be by novel, poem, sermon, or article, has done more, far more, to leaven humanity. I long to open people's eyes to that; I learnt it late myself. Before God, if I can I will make this boy enlightened, should I live to do it; or at least not at the mercy of every vagrant prophet and bawler of conventional ideas.

"Ever your friend,
"Arthur Hamilton"

The next explains itself.

"Tredennis, September 15.

"My Dear Friend,

"As you write to inquire so affectionately about my health, I think it would be very wrong of me not to answer you fully; so I will take 'health' to mean well-being, and not confine myself to its paltry physiological usage.

"In the last month I have really turned a corner, and gained serenity and patience in my outlook. I do not mean that I am either patient or serene yet, but I have long and considerable spaces of both, when I feel content to let God make or mar me as He will, and realise that perhaps in His mind those two words may bear a precisely contrary sense.

"One thing I wish to tell you, which I am afraid you will be rather shocked to hear. I have not told you before, from a culpable reticence; for I believe that there must be either complete confidence between friends or none at all—

"Do you remember a very gloomy and depressed letter that I wrote to you the other day? When I wrote it I was deliberately contemplating an action which I have now given up: I mean a voluntary exit from this world's disappointments—suicide, in fact.

"For many years I have carried about a quietus with me. I began the habit at Cambridge. Men have often asked me what is the curious little flask with a secret fastening, that stands on my dressing-table. It is prussic acid. The morning before I wrote that letter, the impulse was so strong upon me that I determined, if matters should not shift a little, to take it on the following evening. I made, in fact, most methodical arrangements. I seemed so completely to have missed my mark. The superstitions against the practice I did not regard, as they are merely the produce of a more imaginative and anxious system of morality. I did not see why God, for His own purposes— and, what is more, I believe He does—should not remove a man by suicide, if He allows him to die by a horrible disease or relegates him to insanity. Suicide is only a symptom of a certain pitch of mental distress: its incidental result is death, but so it is of many practices not immoral.

"It required considerable nerve, I confess, to make the resolution; but once made, I did not flinch. I considered the impulse to be a true leading, quite as true as the other intuitions which I have before now successfully followed, so I made my arrangements all day. It gave me a wonderful sense of calm and certainty—there was a feeling of repose about the completion of a restless existence, as if I was at last about to slide into quiet waters, and be taught directly, and not by obscure and painful monitions.

"At nine o'clock I went to my room. There was a full moon, which shone in at the open window; the garden was wonderfully still and fragrant.

"I found myself wondering whether, when the thing was over, I should awake to consciousness at once; whether the freed soul would have, so to speak, a local origin, a *terminus a quo*: in plain words, whether my spirit would pass through the house and through the quiet garden to some mysterious home, taking in the earthly impression as it soared past with a single complete undimmed sense—or whether I should step, as it were, straight into a surrounding sea of sensation and be merged at once, feeling through all space and time and matter by the spiritual fibres of which I should make a part. Do you understand me? I have often wondered at that.

"At last I drew out the flask, and touched the spring. It opens by pressing a penknife into one of a number of rivets; you can then unscrew it.

"When it was open I discovered that the little vial inside had been broken, and that somehow or other the life-giving fluid had evaporated unperceived. I had not opened it for a year or more.

"I saw at once that God intended it not to be at *my* time—that was very clear; and after considerable reflection and a wakeful night, I came to the conclusion that my divine Impulse did not lead me to adopt a course of action, but only to *avoid* a course—the fact which I developed in my letter to you. And then came the resolve, tardy and weak at first, but gaining ground, warning me that perhaps it was an inglorious flight; though I knew it was pardonable, I felt as if God might meet me with 'Not wrong, but if you are really bent on the highest, you must do better than this.' It might, I felt, be losing a great opportunity—the opportunity of facing a hopeless situation, a thing I had never done.

"And so I came to the conclusion to fight on, and my reward is coming slowly; contentment seems to return, and Edward is an ever-increasing joy; he fills my life and thoughts. Oh, if I can only make him good; put him in the way of inward happiness! I break out into prayer and aspirations for him in his presence when I think of the utterly heedless way in which he regards the future, and the awful, the momentous issues it contains. He, dear lad, thinks nothing of it, except as a sign of my love for him. We have no misunderstandings, and I seem somehow to love the world better, more passionately, since he came to me.

"I send you a few flowers from our garden, and Edward sends his love, if that is respectful enough.

"I am your affectionate friend, "Arthur Hamilton."

CHAPTER XI

Down at Tredennis the year begun to fly with the speed of which uneventful enjoyable monotony alone possesses the secret.

"Our days are very similar here, and I find them very agreeable. Edward thinks the same, he assures me, though I feel it may arise in his case from a want of breadth of view and lack of experience to argue from.

"In the summer months we get up early, and generally bathe in the stream, where I have contrived to get one of the pools sufficiently enlarged; as the weather gets colder I am compelled by my doctor to relinquish this. Then we read and write till breakfast, which we have at eight o'clock. In winter this is the first event of the day; in the morning we work for an hour or two and then go out, returning to lunch; after which we sun ourselves till five o'clock, or drive; and then, after tea, work again for three hours: the day thus concludes.

"I certainly don't coddle my boy, and I don't think I pet him, for I have the deepest horror of that practice: nothing is so weakening for both parties; it develops sentimentalism, and all mawkishness I abhor!—though I am what you would call ridiculously fond of him. However, you must come and see us, and give me your most candid opinion, criticism, and censure on my educational methods.

"We drive into Truro once a week to market, and Edward goes in on messages, and for some mathematical training to the clergyman there. I should like to find some *æqualis* to make a companion for him. He is English enough for anything, but I am afraid of his not keeping his appropriate boyishness if he is always hanging about with an old and serious valetudinarian like myself. But I don't like any of the families hereabouts, and can't get to know the ones I *do* like well enough to find some one to my mind. I am very fastidious about my selection."

And again:

"Our Sundays are very peaceful days in this lazy land of the West. We go to church—a very necessary part of an Englishman's education—lunch immediately, and then loaf on the downs over the creek, and I read to him till he yawns or goes to sleep; then we both play with Flora among the heather—or botanize—and go to church again."

This letter led me, knowing as I did how pronounced Arthur's views were, to ask him why he took Edward to church, and the line that he intended to take with him generally with regard to religious matters.

"I have given the question," he writes, "a great deal of thought, and feel my way fairly clear now. Ideally, as an experiment, I should like to tell a boy nothing about religion—teach him merely his moral duty—till he is of age; then put the Bible into his hands. There would be, of course, a great deal—the 'purely mythological or Herodotean element,' as Strauss calls it—and the miraculous element generally, that he would probably at first reject; but if he was of an appreciative nature—and I am presupposing that, because I don't think the theory of education is for the apathetic and unsensitive—he would see, I believe, not only the extraordinary sublimity of language and expression, but the unparalleled audacity and magnificence of thought and aspiration. That he would realize the points in which these conceptions were wild, deficient, or childish, would not blind him, I think, to the grandeur of the other side.

"As a matter of fact, we mix up moral duty with intellectual and spiritual so clumsily, and force it so inopportunely and immaturely upon our children, that if in later years questionings begin to arise, or complications in any part of life, the smash that follows is terrific: the whole thing goes by the board.

"For instance: many a man who undergoes a moral conversion will reject his whole intellectual growth angrily and contemptuously as savoring of the times of vanity. In my scheme such a waste would be impossible; the two would be on different planes and not inextricably intertwined.

"Besides, I think that young men suffer terribly from the shock inflicted on their affection and traditional sentiment.

"They grow up with certain stereotyped conceptions on religious subjects, certain dogmas imperfectly understood but crudely imagined and gradually crystallized into some uncouth shape.

"The prejudices of children, and ideas that have grown with them, are, I think, ineradicable in many cases.

"Let us take three instances of such ordinary conceptions—'Grace,' 'the Resurrection of the Body,' 'The Holy Spirit.'

"Here are three vast conceptions. The anxious parent endeavours to explain them to the child: who, in his turn, receives three grotesque and whimsical ideas which represent themselves to him something in the following shape:

"*Grace*. The quality which he detests in his schoolfellows; in which the 'model boys' are pre-eminent; which he knows he dislikes and loathes, and yet is rather ashamed to say so. The boy who 'rebukes' his schoolfellows for irreverent or loose conversation, the boy who is always ready in his odious way to do a kindness, the boy who is never late for school—these seem to him to be the kind of figures that the clergyman is holding up in his sermon as ideal types of character, to be imitated and reverenced, and for whom he has in his young soul the most undisguised and wholesome loathing.

"Of course it is a misconception—but whose fault? Do you blame a tender wayward mind for not having a philosophical grasp of the ideal? Whereas, if you weren't ashamed to let him understand that the young rascal who is always in mischief and behindhand with his work, but who is yet affectionate, generous, and pure, though he is quarrelsome and not particular in his talk, is a far finer fellow, both in point of view of this world and the next than the smooth-faced prig who thanks his Lord that he is not as this publican.

"*The Resurrection of the Body*. Intelligent people who are also reverent and good, in their anxiety to be faithful to the letter of dogma as well as to its spirit, prefer to cling to these words rather than confess, what is quite certain, that an absolutely literal sense was attached to these words by the framers of them; they were scientifically ignorant of the fact that matter is disintegrated and disseminated so rigorously that there may be component particles of a hundred of his predecessors in one human body now existent. No symbolical *interpretation* of the words nowadays will account for their being the expression of what was erroneously believed to be a possibility; and to say, as I have heard a Church dignitary of poetical and metaphysical mind say, that the phrase means that the power resident in every individuality to assimilate to itself certain particles will not desert the individuality even after death, but will continue to assert itself in some way—possibly in a spiritual or unmaterial manner—to say this, is to state a strong scientific probability; but, after all, it is only a probability at best, and is certainly not what the words as they stand in the Creed were meant to mean by the persons who framed them and the first worshippers who repeated them. In the case of children the effect is at once laughable and lamentable. They are made to retain the phrase; no explanation is offered, and, if sought for, shirked. And so it resolves itself into a wonder, dimly conscious of profanity, as to whether Tim Jones the carpenter with the wooden leg, will have a new one; and whether papa will have the wart on his cheek or not, and how he will look without it. Of course these are elementary speculations; but they are true ones, for they were literally my own at an early age. Such speculations are certainly better avoided; and, indeed, all early speculation on dogmatic questions at all is better not suggested.

"*The Holy Spirit*. When I was a child, the dogma of the Trinity caused me the most terrible perplexity, which was all the more distressing because it was shrouded in a kind of awful remoteness, by the reticence, the bewildered and serious reticence, with which my elders approached the subject; but besides the identification with and the appearance as a dove, the term Comforter—and Paraclete, as some of the hymn-books had it—the expression, '*proceeding from* the Father and the Son,' mystified me completely. The three aspects of the central Unity—God as Creator, as the Ideal of Humanity, as the Inspirer of it—is a very subtle and advanced idea; yet it is maintained that symbols should be taught first, before they are understood, so that gradually the growing mind should come to realize and appropriate what it already knows.

"This is a very sophistical and ingenious defence. But it seems to break down in practice. How many people reject the idea when realized, simply, as I hold, on account of the grotesque and fantastic conceptions that the immature and overstrained mind collected about it—conceptions which no amount of *reason* is later able to overcome! And how many never grow to realize it at all! Besides, even of those who do, it is admitted that almost all need a reconstruction *some time*, a breaking-up of what would otherwise be crystallized formulæ, a *conversion*, in fact. Have you ever seen a high nature grow up from boyhood to manhood in undisturbed possession of a vital faith? I confess that I never have!

"I can not help feeling a dismal possibility, that future students of religion, looking over a nineteenth century 'child's catechism,' will laugh, or rather drop their hands in blind amazement—for in truth it is no laughing matter—at the metaphysical conglomerate of dogma, driven like a nail into the heads of careless and innocent children (such, at least, as have had, like myself, the advantage of a religious bringing-up), just as we turn over with regretful amusement and pathetic wonder the doctrinal farrago of a Buddhist or a Hindu.

"And all this because people can't wait. He must have a 'dogmatic basis,' they say, the sinew and bone of religion, when the poor child's head can not even take in their ideas, let alone his emotion appreciate them.

"The consequence is, that I can't bring myself to use these words except in societies where I know I shall not be misunderstood.

"Influence, the indestructibility of matter, aspiration—those are what Grace, the Resurrection of the Body, the Holy Spirit mean to me now; great and living and integral parts of my creed, which I not only glow to reflect about, but which surround and penetrate my life daily and hourly with ever-increasing thankfulness.

"Yet, on the other hand, some people depend so much on tradition: they never have a reconstruction of ideas; memories and associations are all in all to them. They are the 'Bands' people of my former classification.

"And so I want to give Edward both. I take him to church. When he asks me questions I will answer them, but I am glad to say he does not at present. I send him out before the sermon: that is responsible for a good deal of harm. 'Ye shall call upon him to avoid sermons' should be in the rubric of *my* baptismal service.

"Then we read some of the Old Testament history as 'history of the Jews,' and Job and Isaiah and the Psalms as poetry—and I am glad to say he is very fond of them; and parts of the Gospels in Greek, as the life and character of a hero. It is the greatest mistake to impose them upon children as authoritative and divine all at once. It at once diminishes their interest: we ought to work slowly up through the human side.

"The Pauline Epistles I have given him to read in extracts. I believe they are best in extracts—one can omit the controversial element. And he has taken, as children do, to the Revelation enormously, and gets much mysterious delight from it.

"A long and wearisome letter this, and not, I feel, satisfactory. I haven't done justice to the side of tradition, the *jussum et traditum*, but that is the fault of my mind. I have only been professing to represent the other side.

"I would like to thrash the matter out further. I wish you would come down and see us. Tredennis has a sombre beauty, even in winter—a 'season of mists' with us. The magnolia on the south wall is blooming, though we are only two days off Christmas. Our love to you.

"Arthur Hamilton."

I subjoin another extract, on the education of the moral faculty.

"I have always held that the concentration of thought upon morality is a very dangerous system of life. Morality should be an incidental basis to life, not to be brooded over unless some grave disorder should arise. We breathe, and eat, and sleep, and pay no heed to those processes; and indeed both physiologists and moralists exclaim, in the case of those natural processes, that the healthier we are the more unconscious will those processes be.

"So it should be with moral things. If a grave obstruction or contradiction befall any one; if he behaves in a way that violates his usefulness, or his own or others' self-respect; then, if he will not reform himself, we must warn him, or treat him as a physician would: but to abuse a healthy nature for not considering the reasons of things, not having a moral system, not 'preparing for death,' when, by the very constitution of his nature, he does not require one, is a very grave blunder. Moral anxiety is a sign of moral *malaise,* or, far more commonly, a sign of physical disorder.

"It is an ascertained fact that those periods when morals have been imposed on man as his sole and proper business and subject for contemplation have been unprogressive, introspective, feeble times.

"No, leave morals out of the question directly, unless you see there is grave cause for interference. Give one or two plain warnings, or rather commands.

"Try to raise the *tone* generally; try to make the young soul generous, ardent, aspiring. If you can do that, the fouler things will fall off like husks. Above all things, make him devoted to you—that is generally possible with a little trouble; and let him never see or hear you think or say a low thought, or do a sordid thing. If he loves you he will imitate you; and while the virtuous habit is forming, he will have the constant thought, 'Would my father have done this? What would he say, how would he look, if he could see me?' Imagination is sometimes a saving power."

I venture to insert a letter in which he touches delicately on the subject of sexual sin. He would never speak of it, but this was written in answer to a definite question of mine apropos of a common friend of ours.

"I must confess that I do not realize the strength of this particular temptation, but I am willing to allow for its being almost infinitely strong. I don't know what has preserved me. It is the one thing about which I never venture to judge a man in the least, because, from all I hear and see, it must hurry people away in a manner of which those who have not experienced it can not form any conception.

"You ask me what I think the probable effect that yielding to such temptation has on a man's character. Of course, some drift into hopeless sensualists. About those I have my own gospel, though I do not preach it; it is a scarcely formulated hope. But of those that recover, or are recovered, all depends upon the kind of repentance. The morbid repentance that sometimes ensues is very disabling. All dwelling on such falls is very fatal:

all thoughts of what might have been, all reflections about the profaned temple and the desecrated shrine, though they can not be escaped, yet must not be indulged. I always advise people resolutely to try and forget them in *any* possible way—banish them, drown them, beat them down.

"But a manly repentance may temper and brace the character in a way that no other repented fall can. It is the brooding natures which make me tremble; in healthier natures it is the refiner's fire which stings and consecrates: '*Sanat dum ferit.*'

"But the subject is very repugnant to me. I don't like thinking or talking about it, because it has its other side; the thought of a woman in connection with such things is so unutterably ghastly; it is one of the problems about which I say most earnestly 'God knows.'"

One other letter of this period, is worth, I think, inserting here.

"Tredennis, August 29.

"I had an instructive parable thrown in my way to-day, containing an obvious lesson for Eddy, and a further meaning for myself. Eddy came running to me about eleven, to tell me there was a man in the garden. I hurried to the spot he indicated; and there, in a kind of nook formed by a fernery, his head resting in a great glowing circle of St. John's wort, and his feet tucked up under him, lay a drunken tramp, asleep. He was in the last stage of disease; his face was white and fallen away, except his nose and eyes, which were red and bloodshot; he had a horrible sore on his neck; he was unshaven and fearfully dirty; he had on torn trousers; a flannel shirt, open at the neck; and a swallow-tail coat, green with age, buttoned round him. His hat, such as it was, lay on the ground at his side. Edward regarded him with unfeigned curiosity and dismay. While we stood watching him, he began to stir and shift uneasily in his sleep, as a watched person will, and presently woke and rolled to his feet with a torrent of the foulest language. He was three-parts drunk. He watched us for a moment suspiciously, and then gave a bolt. How he accomplished it I don't know, for he was very unsteady on his feet; but he got to the wall, and dropped over it into the road, and was out of sight before we could get there. He evidently had some dim idea that he had been trespassing.

"Edward inquired what sort of a man he was.

"'An English gentleman, in all probability,' I said, 'who has got into that state by always doing as he liked.' And I went on to point out, as simply as I could, that everybody has two sets of desires, and that you must make up your mind which to gratify early in life, determining to face this kind of ending if you fix upon one set. 'Early in life,' I said, 'when this gentleman was a well-dressed clean boy like you, one of the voices used to whisper to him at his ear, "Eat as much as you can; that is what you really like best;" while the other said, "If you eat rather less, you will be able to play football, or read your book better; besides, you will be your own master and less of a beast."

"'But he wouldn't listen; and this is the result.'

"Edward seemed to ponder it deeply. He tried to starve himself to-day at lunch; and I refrained from pointing out to him that abstinence from meat at lunch was not the *unum necessarium*, for fear of confusing the ingenuous mind. I like to see people grasp the concrete issue in one of its bearings. The principle will gradually develop itself; from denying themselves in one point, they will or may grow to be generally temperate; when confronted with overmastering and baser impulses, it may be they will say, 'Let me be ἐγκρατὴς ἐμαυτοῦ even here.'

"So much for Edward's lesson; now for my own. My first impulse was to loathe and reject the poor object, body and soul. He was merely the embodiment of long-continued vice. His body was a diseased framework, breaking quickly up, conscious of no pleasure but appetite, and now merely existing and held together by the desire of gratifying it; the little vitality it possessed, just gathering enough volume in the quiet intervals to satiate one of its three jaded cravings—lust, hunger, and thirst, and feebly groping after alcoholic and other stimulants to repair its exhaustion; the soul in her dreamy intervals drowsily recounting or contemplating lust past and to come—a ghastly spectacle!

"And yet I am bound to think, and do record it as my deliberate belief, that that poor, wretched, withered, gross soul is destined to as sure a hope of glory as any of us: ay, and may be nearer it, too, than many of us, as it is expiating its willfulness in more terrible and direct punishment. There is not a single spasm in that decayed and nerveless frame, not a single horror of all the gloomy forebodings and irrational shudderings of the sickening delirium, not a single mile of the grim dusty roads he wearily traverses, which is not needed to bring him to the truth. The soul may be so clouded that it may not even be taking note of its punishment, may not be even conscious of it, may hardly calculate how low it has fallen and how wretched and hopeless the remainder of its earthly days are bound to be; but I assert that it is none of it blind suffering; that not a pang is unintentionally given, or thrown away; that I shall hand-in-hand with that soul go some day up the golden stairs that lead to the Father, and we shall say one to another, 'My brother, you despised me on earth; you took for a mark of the neglect and disfavour of God what was only a sign of His constant care; you took for an indwelling of foul spirits what was only a testimony of my distance from the truth.'

"And we shall speak together of new things, so marvellous that they will banish memory for ever.

"Who would have thought that the sight of a drunken tramp in a hedgerow would have brought one so close to a sight of God's purposes?

"Yet so it is, my friend. God keeps showing me by the strangest of surprises that He is all about us. This very incident, so seemingly trivial, is yet a part of my life already, it has set its mark upon me. All his life he has been led, from bad to worse, into drink, and haunted by all the other devils of sin, and piloted across the country thus, so that the lines of our lives cut at this instant never to cut again. There are no such things as *chance* meetings. There is no smaller or greater in the sight of God. It is as much a purpose of his life that he should preach this sermon to Edward and myself to-day, as that he should be shown by God's own strokes what happiness really is, by the strong contrast of the bitterness of sin."

The idea of the purpose of God underlying every incident, however apparently trivial, was much in his thoughts just then.

"We often are taught how momentous every thing and every moment is, by the charging of some trivial incident with tremendous issues. A man fires off his gun. He has done so thousands of times already, and yet, like Mr. Jamieson, my neighbour, on this one January morning he kills his own son, converting in a single instant, by a trivial incident, the whole of the rest of his life from sweet into bitter, by the terrible punishment which falls upon 'carelessness.' God seems to be asking us to weigh the fact, that in a chain of events the tiniest link is every bit as important and necessary in its place as the largest.

"And so I begin to take more and more account of little things. The very people we pass in the street once, it may be never to pass again, the stream of faces that flows past us in London—has all that no real connection with our life, except to stir a faint and vague emotion about the size of life and our own infinitesimal share in it? I think it must be something more. Of course, one lets drop grain after grain of golden truth that God slips into our hands. I keep feeling that if we could only truly yield ourselves up for a single instant, put ourselves utterly and wholly in God's hands for a second, the meaning of the whole would flash upon us, and our lesson would be learnt. I think perhaps that comes in death. I remember the only time I took an anæsthetic (when the body really momentarily dies—that is, the functions are temporarily suspended), the great sensation was, after a brief passage of storm and agony, the sense of serenity and repose upon a lesson learnt, a truth grasped, so remote and so connected with infinite ideas, that the coming back into life was like the waking after years of experience; a phantom emotion, I expect; but, like many phantoms, a very good copy of the real one. That is what I expect dying to be like.

"I was going to say that I try not to let even little things—things that are thrust in my way curiously and without apparent reason that is—go uninterpreted. Why should I, for instance, have been introduced by my clergyman to the friend who was staying with him this morning, when I met them in the lane? and why should he have come in to lunch, and talked dull and trivial talk till three o'clock, and interrupted all our plans? There seems some design in it all; and yet one is so impotent to grasp what it can be.

"Yet I suppose no one has failed to notice several small coincidences in their lives, of what might almost be called a providential kind.

"I read in a book about Laennec's method, without the vaguest idea of who Laennec was, or what his method was. The next day, I see, in a chart in the village school-room, 'Laennec, inventor of the stethoscope;' and, the day following, I find and read his biography in a volume that I happen to take up to pass five minutes. And yet we say 'by chance.'

"Or I come across an expression of which I haven't grasped the precise meaning, 'gene,' let us say, or 'eclectic,' and the next day I hear the rector and curate discussing them. These are real cases.

"Or I am interrupted in my writing by Edward, who takes the letters to the post, and forces this from under my hand, as I write: not, surely, only to spare you the receipt of a dull and immature letter.

"Arthur Hamilton."

I have only one other letter of any especial interest about this date.

"If only a book could be written about a hermit, a man that deliberately left the world, retiring, not to an impracticable distance—let us say to a small farm, in a country village, with half an acre of garden—and there let no sound from the world without reach him, except incidentally, and lived a pure and uncontaminated life, watching his garden, and turning over, very slowly, such experience as he had gained in life, with the intention, if anything came of it, of telling the world any solution that occurred to him of the great question—'Is one bound to meet life in the ordinary manner, by plunging into it and swimming up the stream, or does one meet it best by abjuring it?' There is much to be said for both views. I am not at all sure that these or similar lives are not lived, and that the only practical bearing of them is that a man is *not* bound to tell his discoveries of our enigmas. I mean, I can conceive a man, under such circumstances, reaching a very high standpoint, arriving at very lofty knowledge of the problems of fate and life, and at the same time finding a ban laid upon him, a tacit ἀνάγκη, not to reveal it to others, it being hinted to him that those who would attain to it at all must attain to it as he has himself attained, by finding out the way themselves."

CHAPTER XII

About this time he made the acquaintance of some neighbours whom he approved, and found companions for Edward Bruce in the boys of the family, who were home for the holidays. The boy brightened up so much under the new surroundings, that Arthur determined to get a boy of the same age to educate with Edward, and he accordingly inserted an advertisement in the *Times*. I have it before me now, in the fast-yellowing paper.

"A gentleman is anxious to find a companion to be educated with his adopted son; he offers him board and teaching free, but must see, personally, both the parent or guardian and the boy whom it is proposed to send."

But the advertisement was withdrawn, as a friend of mine, a certain General Ellis, not very well off, and with a large family, offered to send a boy of his to Tredennis—an offer which Arthur accepted provisionally. He had the boy to stay with him for a fortnight, and at the end of the time agreed to take him.

As the boys were not to go to a public school, and as neither of them looked forward to teaching as a career, the object of their teaching was to make them as quick in grasp of a subject as possible, as enthusiastic as possible, and as cultivated. Arthur favoured me with a letter, or rather a treatise, upon their education, fragments of which I submit to my readers.

"My aim will be to make them, generally speaking, as adequate as possible to playing a worthy part in the world. I want them to be as open-minded on all subjects as possible, to have no fixed prejudices on any subject, and yet to have an adequate basis of knowledge on important matters, enough not to leave them at the mercy of any new book or theory on any subject which handles its facts in at all a one-sided way—so that on reading a brilliant but narrow book on any point, they may be able to say, 'This and that argument have weight, they are valid; but he has suppressed this, and distorted that, which, if seen fairly and in a good light, would go far to contradict the other.' Then they must be without *prejudice*; they must not close their eyes or turn their backs on any view, because it is 'dangerous' or 'damaging' or 'subversive' or 'unpractical.' They must not be afraid to face an idea because of its probable consequences if its truth is proved. They must not call anything common or unclean.

"For this they must have a basis of knowledge on these points; history, political economy, philosophy, science. The first three I am fairly competent to give them; that is to say, I am studying these hard myself now, and I can, at any rate, keep well ahead of them; and I have managed to win their educational confidence, which is a great thing. They take for granted that a thing which is dull is necessary, and follow me with faith; while, I am thankful to say, they are keen enough not to want driving when a thing is interesting.

"Then they must know French and German, and a modicum of Greek and Latin. These last I teach them by a free use of translations; rudiments of grammar first, and then we attack the books, and let grammar be incidental. We don't compose in any of these languages; it's a mere waste of time.

"I teach them logic and Euclid, and get them taught some mathematics. Then as to science, by reading myself with them we get on very well together. And I have bought a few chemicals, and we try experiments freely, which is very satisfactory.

"Music I teach them both, and harmony. They don't much like it, but they will be glad some day. I make them practise regularly. I don't believe any but very exceptionally gifted boys like that; but they are so awfully thankful when they get to my age if they have been kept at it.

"Then as to the external παιδεία, there is my difficulty. I am not allowed to take any active exertion myself, and, indeed, it tells on me if I do, so that I have become a kind of thermometer, hopeless and headachy and listless the next day, if I overdo myself the very least; so that I have merely to encourage them by precept, not by example. They have ponies and bicycles, and scamper about all over the country. Edward has been brought home once in a cart, but not seriously damaged; and I like to leave them to themselves in these things—they won't damage themselves a bit the less for fussing and fretting over them, and they will lose ever so much independence and go. Then I teach them to shoot, and they are very fair shots with a pea-gun. And we also do a little carpentering, so we are well employed. They aren't showy performers at any game, but, as they won't be at school, that makes very little difference to them; it is handiness in general sports that is valuable afterward.

"You would think that this was a tremendous programme, but it is not; it is mostly reading and talking, with a certain amount of writing. They have to analyse a chapter of a book of some kind every day; sometimes history, sometimes philosophy. We do both history and philosophy as much as possible by means of biographies. Lewes's book is an excellent text-book, and not a bit too advanced if you will talk it over with them carefully; clever boys are never really puzzled by meanings of words. In history we get the greatest man we can find in a period, and work out his view of all current events; and they have to write dialogues in character, and enjoy it immensely too. I don't press them to read for themselves very much, and I don't make ordinary English literature their task-books, because one always may be boring a boy, and I don't want to run the risk of boring them with things that I want them to enjoy as much as I did.

"I read to them for an hour or so every evening—novels, plays, anything that they seem to like. They are at liberty to choose.

"I don't know that they would 'go down' at present—certainly not among their compeers. They talk quite naturally and straightforwardly about all kinds of topics of general interest, and they are tremendously keen about their games, but I think some people might call them prigs. However, I keep them in a constant and wholesome contempt of their own abilities, and never let them despise or criticize anyone unfavourably; not by 'rebuking' it, but by indicating a point of view—and one can always find one—in which the person under fire is infinitely their superior.

"And they are as affectionate as they can be—they like one another and me; and they aren't easily disturbed by circumstances, not having had their morbid sensibilities developed, their innocent perceptions dimmed by alcoholic or other dissipations."

I select, rather at random, one or two other passages from his letters at this time.

"I have just been reading Emerson's Essays. They certainly kindle one's belief in the greatness of life and the nobility of little things; but, after all, the great refreshment of such books to me is—not that they give me new working ideas; I hardly know a book that has ever done that; the stock of ideas is almost constant in the world; but because they show that others are on the same track of admiration and hope as one's self for a goal only hinted at and conjectured to be glorious—on the same track, and farther advanced upon it; like older people, they fill in with experience what one has only guessed at. I find myself saying, 'I expect that life will be like this and that: it will confirm this and that idea in startling ways:' and then one of these great souls comes softly to me, and says, 'It is true.'"

And again:

"There are a great number of conventional ideas which are largely current, not only conversationally and among ordinary people, but in books—good and sensible books, written by people of experience—which are, in my opinion, radically and absolutely false, and yet no one takes the trouble to question them. I am always coming across them. Such as this: *No one is more incapable of affection than a profligate.* This, in my judgement, is a ludicrous error, though it is the statement of no less a moral physician than Lacordaire. If by affection you mean 'sustained, pure, disinterested emotion,' such as patriotism—well and good; but affection!—the two most affectionate persons I have ever known were thoroughly dissolute; and I mean by affection, not a slobbering sentimental passion of a purely sensual type, but an affection quite untainted, to all appearances leading them to make considerable sacrifices for the sake of it, and causing them the acutest misery when not reciprocated. In so far as profligates are selfish brutal natures, as they often are, it is true; but that is not the case with half of them. They are not unfrequently people of infirm will, strong affections, and a violent animal nature. It is selfishness, regard to personal *comfort* at all hazards, which is the hopeless nature, and can not be raised except through pain.

"Speaking of Lacordaire, another favourite position of his will illustrate my point. He was constantly inveighing in his seminary against desultory reading. Homer, Plutarch, Racine, Bossuet, and a few other books, are all he wishes a man to have read. He calls miscellaneous reading a subtle dissipation, a moral poison.

"It seems to me to depend entirely upon temperament. Some natures are like *mills*, converting everything that comes in their way into grist; and in that case, no doubt, it is deleterious. They are people of slow-revolving mind, to whom statements in books are of the nature of authorities. Lacordaire was one, I think.

"But there are others who are like sieves; who want a constant passing of materials of all kinds over them to let a little fall through; people who draw from a huge jumble of miscellaneous facts, theories, and thoughts, a little sediment of truth of the precise size to suit them. Such a person was Macaulay.

"I believe that interference does more harm than good. If you thrust books upon a mind of the first type, the result is confusion and weariness. If you deny them to the latter, all you get is poverty of ideas, and morbidity, and mawkishness. I make a rule never to interfere with anybody's reading."

Four years passed. I went during that time once to Tredennis—in the summer, when I took my scanty holiday; for I was in a Government office where only six weeks were allowed. Arthur was generally away in the summer. He took Edward Bruce to several friends' houses; to his own home in Hampshire, now for a long time in the hands of strangers. He wanted to make him a real Englishman. It was arranged that he should go to Cambridge in October. He matriculated at Trinity, Arthur's own college; and he was looking forward with great delight to the prospect.

I went down to stay at Tredennis for a week in July. I got to the house through the quiet sultry lanes about the middle of the afternoon, having started very early from town. As I came up the little drive I could see through the trees an animated game of lawn-tennis proceeding on the lawn in front of the house, between two flannelled combatants. At the sound of the wheels they broke off the game, and Edward came up to greet me. He was now nearly nineteen, and had lost none of the beauty of his boyhood; a small brown moustache which fringed his upper lip being, to my eyes, almost the only sign of his advancing years. He introduced me to his friend, a young Eton man, possessed of that frank nonchalance which it is the privilege of that institution to bestow. I inquired where Arthur was. Edward told me that he had gone down to the stream for a stroll. "We'll go down and find him," he said, putting his arm in mine, with that same demonstrativeness that had always characterized him, and that won people to him so quickly.

We crossed one or two adjacent fields which sloped down to the stream, conspicuous by its fringe of alder and hazel; and after crossing by a gravel-pit, we came on a level reach of it, all stifled with high water-plants, figwort, and loosestrife, and willow-herb, and great sprawling docks, till, down by a little runnel where it took a sudden turn round a shoal of gravel, we came upon the faint fragrance of a cigarette; then Flora ran forward to meet us; and, on turning the corner, we found a great long figure lying on the bank, with hat half pulled over his eyes, gazing dreamily up into the shifting willow leaves and the blue above.

Our voices, which had been drowned by the sound of the running water, aroused him, and he sat up, and, on seeing me, got slowly to his feet with a delightful smile of welcome on his face. "How are you, my dear man?" he said. "I didn't expect you so early, or I should have been at home to meet you—in fact, I should have driven down to Truro, only I am not quite the thing to-day."

I looked rather anxiously at him, to see how he appeared to be, and was much struck with the change in him. There had crept into his face what has been called a look of "doom." The Stuarts are said to have had it. I can not describe it in any other way. It was that of a man waiting for something, bravely and calmly, but still with a certain sort of apprehension. He looked very solemn and grave when he was not speaking, and he was apt to get a kind of brooding look, which did not disperse till one spoke to him. He was thinner, too, and paler, though the old lock of hair still dangled over his forehead, and his eyes had the old affectionate look.

He was playful and humorous in a quiet way. I have forgotten what we talked about—we discussed people and things vaguely; I can only remember one little remark he made which struck me as being highly characteristic. I had said, in reply to some question as to one of our friends, "Oh, he's perfectly crazy." "Yes," said Arthur, mildly: "he has certainly got some curious mannerisms."

I ventured to remonstrate with him about the cigarette, but he said gravely that he had given up thinking about his health, it was so very inferior, and that he had come to the conclusion that nothing in moderation made him either better or worse; "and an occasional cigarette," he said, "adds so much to my general serenity, that I feel sure it is perfectly justifiable."

I had a very delightful week there. He talked a good deal, when he was in the mood, about the books he had been reading and the thoughts he had been thinking; but his physical languor at times, especially in the mornings, was very painful to see. He did not get up till very late, and complained to me more than once of a terrible listlessness and dejection to which he was liable during the earlier part of the day. But he spoke little of his own sufferings, or rather *malaise*, which I gathered was very great, only saying once or twice, "It is fortunate how habituated one gets to things, even to enduring discomfort. If I can only get my mind occupied, it hardly ever distracts me now." And again—"I think the only really valuable experiences are those that we can not lay down and take up at will, but which continue with us, invariable, unaltering, day after day, meeting us at every moment and tempering every mood." And once—"In spite of everything, I would not for an instant go back. I have every now and then, on breezy sunny mornings or after rain, an intense gush of yearning for the peculiar unconscious delight—the index of perfect physical health—of childhood; but I never deliberately wish that things were otherwise. I enjoy nature more, far more, than ever I did. The signs of spring are a deep and constant joy to me. I can lie down by the stream, and watch the water flowing and the flowers bending and stirring and the animals that run busily about, and be absolutely absorbed, without a thought of myself or even other people. This I never could do before, and it has been sent me, I often think, as a kind of alleviation. I have had it ever since I settled here at Tredennis; and altogether I feel the stronger and the more content for all this suffering and the inevitable end, which can not be far off. No; I wouldn't change, even with you, my dear Chris, or even with Edward"—as that superb piece of physical vitality crossed the lawn.

"When I first came," he told me, "quite at first, I seemed to have lost my hold of nature—to be discordant and out of joint with her. On those bright still mornings we so often have here in the early summer, I seemed to be only a sad spectator, not a part of it all. The sunset over the hills there, and the deliberate red glow of the creek, all seemed to mock me. Even Edward, fond as he was of me, seemed to have no real connection with me. I was isolated and despairing. But very gradually, like the dispersing of a cloud, it came back. I began again to feel myself a performer in the drama, not a gloomy spectator of it—there must be the sufferer, the condemned, to make the tragedy complete, and they may be enacted well—till the sense of God's Fatherhood came back to me. So that I can be and feel myself a part of the vast economy, diseased and inefficient though I am—feel that I am one with the life that throbs in the trees and water, and that forces itself up at every cranny and nestles in every ledge—can wait patiently for my move, the transference of my vital energy—as strong as ever, it seems to me, though the engines are weaker—to some other portion of the frame of things."

He spoke of spiritualism with great contempt. "The more I see of spiritualists and the less I see of phenomena," he said, "the more discontented with it I am. It is nothing but a fashionable drawing-room game."

He dwelt a good deal on the subjective interpretation of nature. One evening—we had been listening to the owls crying—he said, abstractedly:

"We put strange meanings enough, God knows, into faces that never owned them. We hear dreary hopelessness in the moaning of the wind; wild sorrow in the tossing of the trees; and read into the work-a-day cries of birds, content, humour, melancholy, and a thousand other unknown feelings."

He spoke much about the country and its effect on people. "Wisdom," he said, "is generally reared among fields and woody places, and when she is nearly grown she wanders into the cities of men, to see if she can not rule there; and then the test really comes. If she is genuine and strong, she says her say and makes her protest, and passes back again, uncontaminated, into the quiet villages, as pure and free as ever. That is the case with genius. But if the spring of her energy is not all her own—is not quite untainted, she parts with her old grace and glory, losing it in hard unloving talk, in selfish intercourse, in striving after the advantages of comfort and wealth. She stays, and is dissipated—she is conformed to the image of the world. That is what happens to mere talent."

The only other conversation with him that impressed itself very distinctly upon my mind was about religion. He had been thinking—so he told me—very deeply about Christianity, its strength and weakness. "Its weakness, nowadays," he said, "is the mistake of confusing it with the principles advocated by any one of the bodies that profess to represent it. When one sees in the world so many bodies—backed by wealth, tradition, prestige—shouting, 'We are the only authorized exponents of Christ's truth; we are the only genuine succession of the apostles;' when we see Churches who claim and make much of possessing the succession (which they have in reality forfeited by secession), and yet demand the right to be heretical if the main stream is, as they say, 'corrupted' (for once introduce that principle, and you can never limit subdivision, and equitable subdivision too)—it is no wonder weaker intellects are confused and distressed, and from their inability to decide between five or six sole possessors of the truth, fall outside teaching and encouragement altogether, though they could have got what they wanted in any of these bodies.

"But, in spite of the hopeless strife of Churches, the fundamental attraction of Christianity for human nature remains every bit as strong—to be able to say to all people, 'Imagine and idealize the best human being possible; put into him all the best qualities of all the best people you have ever known—give him strength, sympathy, power beyond the most powerful on earth, and add to that a great deep individual affection for *you yourself*, of a kind that is never moved by insults, or chilled by coldness, or diverted by ingratitude;'—say to them, 'And he has been waiting quietly for you for years, for the least sign of affection on your part, never disgusted, never impatient, always ready to turn and welcome you.'

"Think what a hold you establish, saying this, over all people conscious of unhappiness of any kind, over all those refined natures coarsening under a vile *entourage*, over all unsatisfied hearts craving for a friend that their surroundings can not give them, over all who have lost delight for whatever cause in common familiar things, and have nowhere to turn. When one reflects how many human beings fall under one or other of these heads, one does not wonder at it."

I returned to London, feeling wonderfully refreshed and invigorated, both in body and mind, by my visit. Then, as ever, I could not help feeling a subtle influence in Arthur's conversation and presence, that defied analysis and yet was undoubtedly there. He seemed to encourage one to hope, or rather believe, in the ultimate tendency to good in all things, to wait and watch the developments and the bents of life, rather than to fret over particular events—and this without a vague optimism that refuses to take count of what is unsatisfactory and foul, but looking causes and consequences fairly in the face. "I never quite understood the parable of the tares," he said to me, just before I went, "till I found these words in a book the other day: 'The root of the common darnel (*lolium*) or dandelion, with saltpeter, make a very cheap and effective sheep-drench. It can be applied successfully in cases of fluke.'"

In October, 1883, as had been arranged, Edward went up to Trinity College, Cambridge. I had a short letter from Arthur telling me. It ended characteristically thus: "I don't in the least care that Edward should be distinguished academically. I do care very much what sort of a character he is. What one does, matters so very much less than how one does it. It is the method, not the thing, which shows what the man is. I shall be very much disgusted if he *means* to work and doesn't, but merely drifts; whereas, if he is idle on principle, I don't much care. 'Do what you mean to do,' is what I have always told him. If I hear that he is doing fairly well and making friends, and finds himself at home, I shall be content, but nothing more. But if I hear that he is influential and takes his own line, I shall be very much pleased, even if that line is not quite the most respectable, or that influence is not now for the best."

This letter was dated November 1st. On November the 9th, Edward Bruce was killed by a fall from a dog-cart, driving into Cambridge from Ely. He had driven over there with a friend, a pleasant but somewhat reckless man. They had dined at Ely, and were returning in the evening, both in the highest spirits. Edward was driving; the horse took fright, in a little village called Drayton, at a dog that ran across the road. Edward was thrown out on to his head, and, entangled in the reins, was dragged for some distance. The other escaped with a few bruises.

Arthur was acquainted with the terrible news by telegraph. He came up to Cambridge at once, ill and broken with the shock as he was. They told me that he looked terribly pale, but with a quiet self-possessed manner he made all arrangements and settled all bills. The poor boy was buried in the northwest corner of the cemetery at Cambridge. Arthur put up a little tablet to him at Trinity and at St. Uny Trevise.

In Memory of
E. B.,
BORN AT TEHERAN;
DIED AT CAMBRIDGE, NOV. 9, 1883.
"What I do thou knowest not now, but
thou shalt know hereafter."

Arthur had an interview with Edward's companion on the fatal occasion. I subjoin the latter's account of it. He requested me, when I wrote to him to ask him for some particulars relating to Edward Bruce, to make what use I wished of the letter.

"I can't describe the effect the accident had on me. It half drove me mad, I think. I was very much attached to Edward Bruce, as, indeed, we all were. I don't attempt to condone the fault. It was due entirely to my carelessness. I pressed him to drive faster than he was willing to do. I laughed at his scruples. I whipped the horse on myself. I never clearly knew what happened—for I was stunned myself—till I woke up and was told.

"When Mr. Hamilton came to see me, I was sitting in my room, over my breakfast, which I could not eat. His card was brought in by my gyp, and it made me faint and sick. He came in with his hand out, looking very pale, but smiling just as he used to smile, only more sadly. 'Don't reproach me,' I said; 'I can't bear it.' 'Reproach you!' he said—and I shall never forget the tone of affectionate wonder with which it came, or the relief it was to me to hear it—'Reproach you! I know how you loved him.' I broke down at that, and cried wretchedly. I found him sitting by me. He put his hand on my shoulder and stroked my hair. 'I have only one more thing to say,' he said, at last. 'You will not mind my saying it, will you? Eddy had told me all about you—he was very open with me—that you were not doing justice to your opportunities here, not fulfilling your own ideals and possibilities. All I ask of you is to let this be the impulse to rise; do not let any morbid or fantastic remorse stand in your way, and baffle you. You know that he would have been the first to have forgiven any share of the fault that may be yours. What I wish most earnestly for you—it is what he, if he had lived, would have wished most—is that you should become a nobler man—as you can, I know; as you will, I believe.' I could not speak, or answer him then; but I have tried to do what he begged me. Perhaps you do not know—I hope you do not—what a struggle an attempt to forget is. I could not have believed that a memory could hang so heavily round my neck.

"He wrote to me once after, and sent me Edward's riding-whip and flask. I never saw him again. From what Edward told me, and from the little I saw of him myself, I knew that he was the humblest and gravest of men. In his dealing with me, he showed himself the most truly loving."

I was at Tredennis for a week just after this. At the end of that time he begged me not to stay—he could bear it better alone. My impression was that he was like a man half dazed with grief. He sat very silent, and would do nothing; if he ever spoke, it was with evident effort. He did not appear to be ill, only crushed and overwhelmed. Once he broke down. He was looking over some books, and found a notebook of Edward's, of some subject they had been reading together. Edward had tired of the subject, and the last page was occupied with a pen-and-ink sketch of Arthur himself, the discovery of which, done as it had been during working hours, had been the occasion of some affectionate strictures. He shut the book up quickly, and literally moaned.

Then, after a little, his frosty silence broke up, and he wrote me several letters about his boy, very full and detailed, with numbers of little stories, and ending with a passionate burst of grief at the loss. They are too private for publication.

One very notable one, some six months after, must be given here.

"People talk and write about instantaneous momentary *conversions*—I never realized what was meant till a week ago. Day after day, all that time, I had been filled with gloomy, reproachful, or bitter thoughts of God and the providence which took Edward from me. It was intolerable that he should be swept away into silence, leaving me so worn and hopeless, and, worst of all, so dissatisfied and discontented with the hand that did it—my vaunted philosophy failing and giving out utterly. I *knew* it was right, but could not *feel* it.

"But last night as I sat, as I have so often done, burning and racked with recollection and regret, a kind of peace stole over me. It was quite sudden, quite abnormal; not that afterglow of hope that sometimes follows a dark plunge of despair, but a gentle firm trust that seemed, without explaining, yet to make all things plain; not ebbing and flowing, not changing with physical sensation or mental weariness, but deep, abiding, sustaining. You may think it rash of me thus, after so short an interval, to write so assuredly of it; but even if I lost the sense (and I shall not) the memory of that moment would support me; 'If I go down into hell, thou art there also,' is the only sentence that expresses it.

"But I shall not lose it; it has been with me in many moods—and my moods are many and very variable, as you know. I can't express it in words; but I feel no more doubt about Edward's well-being, no more inclination to fret or murmur, besides an all-embracing and pervading sense of satisfied content that penetrates everywhere and applies itself to everything; those are the chief manifestations.

"It is as if he had come to me himself and whispered that all was well, or, better still, as if the great Power that held both him and me and all men within His grasp, had sent His messenger to strengthen me. My friend, all the struggles and miseries of my life have paled to nothing in the light of this. If this is to be won by suffering, pray that you may suffer; though I feel, indeed, as if I had not earned or deserved a tenth part of it—it is the free gift of God. It is to this that we shall all come."

He still lived at Tredennis; spending much of his time in visiting and talking to the people round about, the cottagers and farmers. He was very weak in the mornings, and mostly read, or often was too feeble even for that; but later in the day his strength used somewhat to revive, and he would walk along the lanes with Flora, now growing older and more sedate, trotting by him. He was known and loved in the circle of the hills. "Oh, sir," as a poor woman said to me, with tears in her eyes, after he was gone, "I can't tell you how it was—he spoke very little of Him—but he seemed to remind me of the Lord Jesus, if I am not wrong to say it, more than all Mr. Robert's sermons or the pictures in the school-house. He was so kind and gentle; he seemed to bring God with him!"

But the end was not far off. He got very much weaker in the spring: he suffered from violent paroxysms of pain, depriving him of sight and power of speech, and wearing him out terribly. On the 21st of April I was telegraphed for; he wished to see me.

I came in the evening; he was conscious, and seemed glad to see me, though he was very weak. He said to me, "When I was at Cambridge, my windows overlooked a space of grass, very evenly green in the spring; but in a hot summer the lines of old foundations and buildings used to come out, burning the grass above them with the heat they retained; it is just the same," he added, "with things that I thought I had forgotten—they come out very truthfully now."

He often spoke to me of his grief that he had never seen Edward's face after he left Tredennis to go to Cambridge, for he had been fearfully disfigured, cut and bruised by the accident, and he had no picture of him; "But perhaps it is because I was too fond of his face," he said.

He had several terrible spasms while I was with him, and the doctor said that if he had such another he could not last out the night. Once, after waking from the prolonged and weary sleep of prostration which used to follow these collapses, he said to me, with a smile, "I saw him."

Once he said, "I have just dreamed of a tall man, who came to me and said, 'You will be surprised when you meet Edward; he is delighting everyone there with his conversation; he is so much wiser; and he has grown so much handsomer," adding, with a smile, "though I still think that an impossibility."

About six o'clock on the morning of the 24th he seemed very uneasy in his sleep. On waking, he said, "I should like to receive the Sacrament."

I confess that I thought that he was wandering; he had given up this religious observance for years. He repeated it, adding, "I am not wandering; I know what I am saying."

I went at once to the rectory. The rector was away, and I was directed to the curate, who lived in the village.

I went straight to him, and made my request. He refused to comply. I will do him the justice to say that he appeared to be profoundly concerned and distressed. "I can't act without my rector in this," he said. "I daren't take the responsibility. He hasn't attended the Communion for years; I know his opinions are distinctly unchristian; and in my last talk to the rector, he confessed to me that if Mr. Hamilton (speaking hypothetically) were to present himself for Communion, he should be obliged to refuse him."

I spoke very hastily, and I think unfairly. Mr. J—— tried to remonstrate, but I would not hear him.

When I came back, Arthur was asleep. As soon as he awoke, before he was quite conscious, he said, "It is like a river; it flows very smoothly, and carries me off my feet; but the sun is on it, and it is very clear."

I told him about the *rencontre*. He smiled faintly, and said, "Ask him to come and see me, at any rate; he can't refuse that." I sent the message at once.

At nine o'clock he had a fearful spasm; so terrible that I could not endure to see it, and left the room. While I was down-stairs, the curate arrived. He had come of his own accord, bringing the vessels with him. It had been, he pleaded, only a momentary hesitation.

In half an hour I was told that he would like to see us. The doctor was with him; as we entered, he told me, "He can not last an hour." Then, to the curate, "You may begin the service, if you like, though I doubt if he can hear you; he certainly will not be able to receive."

He was very gray about the eyes and temples, and looked fearfully exhausted. His eyes were closed. The curate began in a quiet voice, rather agitated. When he was near the end, Arthur opened his eyes fully and saw him. The curate went forward. Arthur held out his hand. "Thank you for coming," he said.

The curate grasped his hand, and said, "Can you forgive me for not coming at once?"

"You were doing your duty," said Arthur; adding, with a half-smile, "and you are doing it now," as he saw the open book.

Then he began to wander. I heard him say this: "He seems to halt. Yes! but it is only seeming."

Then for ten minutes he was very still. Then he gave an uneasy movement, and half raised himself.

"He is going," said the doctor.

Suddenly he opened his eyes. "All three," he said. They were his last words. The curate began to say a prayer; we none of us interrupted him. There was a convulsive movement, and all was over. The doctor went out. We cried like children by the bed.

RECAPITULATION

I had rather intended to say no more; to let the Life speak for itself. I had imagined that a moral destroyed, rather than enhanced, the effect of a story; that a descriptive catalogue rather interfered with one's appreciation of a picture than otherwise; but a friend to whom I showed my little collection, and to whose opinion I greatly defer, expressed surprise at the abruptness of the close. "You seem to leave the end," he said, "tangled and unravelled; one wants the threads just gathered together again." So I will try and discharge this task.

The difficulty is not to arrive at a deterministic theory of life for most men. Anyone who will take things as he finds them, and fairly come to a conclusion about them, not hampered by fetters of authority or tradition, but independently arriving at his own solution, must inevitably arrive at this; there is no logical escape. But the difficulty lies in the application of this determinism to life. So many people persist in saying that it is only a logical account of the existence of the world, only an ontological solution, not a life-philosophy. The best man, who can not confute it, only says mournfully that it will not do for an ethical system; nothing good can come out of it in practice.

The writer is one of those who believe that truth, however painful, is essentially practical. That truth when seen must be applied, must be worked out into life, is his cherished idea. But he, as much as anyone, has felt the usual (alas!) and bitter consequences of determinism; has seen the victim of the thought sit, as it were, with his hands tied; has seen the determinist sink into temporary fatalism, and has seen effort relaxed and ideals growing hourly dim.

He was beginning to suffer in this manner himself when, at Cambridge, he met Arthur; and met in him not only an inspiring acquaintance, an encouraging friend, but a man who was far ahead of him on the same path where he had only ventured to imprint a few trembling footsteps, and then draw back appalled at the sombre prospect. Arthur was like one further up the pass, who had turned a corner, so to speak, and saw the road plain.

He found a thoroughgoing determinist who was still faithful to the voice of duty, still striving upwards; he found that his theories, far from giving him a sense of gloom and hopelessness, rather bestowed on him a frank expectant habit of soul; a readiness to weigh circumstances, however small, to overlook nothing as trivial or common; and a serene trust in an invisible all-ruling Father (παντοκράτωρ, as he used to say), who really was ordering the world in the smallest details when He seemed to be ordering it least, and who wished the best for His children—far better than they had insight to wish for themselves, and who thus could be trusted not to be inflicting any useless blow, any meaningless torment, even when things looked blackest and the world most unintelligible.

I do not maintain that Arthur never flagged or swerved from this; the letter will show it was far otherwise: but this was his deliberate habit of mind; this was the ideal that he was faithful to, with all allowances for a humanity, and a humanity sorely tried.

He was an ambitious man by nature; I am sure of that: *that* he conquered. He was indolent by nature, averse to detail, and motion, and change: *that* he conquered by deliberate rough travel. He disliked new people: *that* he set himself to conquer. In the prime of his life, being of a nature to which health and ordinary enjoyments of life were very delightful and precious, death was suddenly and hopelessly set before him; he loved and was disappointed; and the one charge that was given him, the education of his friend's boy, was overwhelmed and ended in a moment by a little act of boyish carelessness. Keenly sensitive to physical pain, the last years of his life were racked with it, every week, almost every day.

Such are the materials of a life. Apparently self-regarding in idea, and prematurely cut short in fact, it has left results on a small circle of friends that will never die. And why?

Because, in spite of every trial and every rebuff, he preserved at heart a serenity that was not thoughtlessness, a cheerfulness that was not hilarity, a humour that was not cynicism. The biographer has thought fit to give expression to his darkest hours, and they were not few; they may appear in the life to have the preponderance, but he would not cut them out. No life is inspiriting that is not occasionally weak and faulty. What would

David be without his sins; Peter, without his fall? There was no depth of the despairing spirit, I say it deliberately, that Arthur had not sounded — and he had not been, as it were, lowered — deaf, blind, and unconscious — into the abysmal deeps; it was with an eye alert to mark every ledge of the dark walls, an ear quick to catch the smallest murmur from below, a sense keen to experience and record every new depth gained, every qualm of heart-sickness encountered. Naturally prone to serious contemplation of life's enigmas, there was not one that life did not bring with shocking vividness to his touch.

Further, I believe that some will be found to say, "The teaching of this life is so selfish; it is all self-contemplation, miserable self-weariness, gloomy reveries bounded by the narrowest horizons. If ever he turns to others' evil case, it is with the melancholy satisfaction of the hypochondriac, who finds his own symptoms repeated with less or greater variations in others' cases." To these I could only reply, "You have totally misunderstood the life. It is not a selfish one. The deepest self-communings are necessary to one who would know human nature, because self is the only human creature that can be known with a perfect intimacy. 'No one but yourself can tell,' as Arthur once wrote to me, 'what ruled the lines in your face.'" But Arthur, above all others that I have ever known, had passed from the particular to the general. Plato's praise of love was based on the principle that the philosopher passed from the love of one fair form to the love of abstract beauty. The fault is that so many never pass the initiation. Arthur did cross the threshold; he passed from the contemplation of his own suffering to the consideration of the root of all human suffering. He found his best comfort in doing all he could (and God allowed him little latitude) to alleviate the sufferings of others. I have letters from various of his friends, dealing, with his firm and faithful touch, with crisis after crisis in their lives. No one who had trusted him with his confidence once, ever shrank from doing it again. I am forced to admit that, far more than many of his authorized brethren, he discharged the priestly office. He was self-constituted, or rather called, to be a priest of God.

The great mystery of *effectiveness* he never solved, I think, quite to his own satisfaction. His life has solved it for me ever since I was able to regard it *en masse*. It was a great puzzle to him what to make, for instance, of infants who died at or before birth. "'Saved from this wicked world' is such a horrible statement in such cases," he used to say. "If that is the best that can happen to us, what *can* we make of life?" And so he was always very urgent about the influence of example opposed to the influence of precept.

"My father," he said to me, "once spoke to me rather sharply about not attending at family prayers. He did not attend very closely himself. I was an observant boy, and I knew it. The very fact that he should have noticed me proved it. So all I felt was that prayer didn't matter really, but that, however I felt, I must behave as if I was devout; whereas, if he had prayed in rapt fervency, unconscious of anything, I should have been ashamed, I think, to wander. I should have perceived the beauty of prayer. Ah, my dear friend," he added, "never speak to a child about a thing unless you *know* you always do it yourself, and even then with extreme and tender caution."

Acting then, on this principle, he did not give us lectures and rules: but we saw how a man was meeting life, not shirking any of its problems, and beset by most of its trials. And we wondered what was the secret spring of his well-being; and when we came to examine it, we were amazed to find that it was in the strength of principles resulting from a rigid and logical classification of phenomena.

So much is said nowadays about the dissidence of the spiritual and intellectual worlds. Many people, conscious of intellect, are yet strangely at sea when they are told of their *spiritual* side. There appears to be nothing within them answering to that description. There are, indeed, certain qualities or characteristics, but those seem not to exist independent of their intellectual and physical economies, but to permeate both. They do not understand that what is meant is the faculty of emotional generalization. *That* they could understand. Arthur arrived at his principles purely through logical methods and intellectual operations. He could not, he often confessed, separate the intellectual and the spiritual. From some expressions, however, which dropped from him in a letter, I am vaguely aware that he was reconsidering that point (and it has been suggested to me that such an explanation will suit his last words); but, in any case, he was of the greatest possible comfort to us who knew him, because he was an instance (the only one) of a man who had arrived at his principles from a purely intellectual basis.

And let me, finally, correct the impression, if I have by chance, in developing this latter point, given any colour to the idea that his character was hard, logical, unaffectionate, unloving. Arthur was the tenderest, most sympathetic, most loving soul I have ever met; nothing else would explain his influence. He was not demonstrative, and was often misunderstood. His tendency was to dissimulate the strongest of his feelings. Yet I have seen him turn red and pale at the sight of a letter in the handwriting of a friend he loved; I have seen him literally tremble with emotion when Edward Bruce, in his impulsive boyish way, would, with eager demonstrative affection, throw his arm round his neck, or take his hand. The tears gather in my eyes as I write, when I recall a few words of his a few days before he died, when he called me to him. It was after one of those terrible paroxysms of pain. He was very white and feeble, but smiling. He took my hand, and said, "What a wonderful thing it is that pain takes away one's power of thinking of anything except people. It hurries one away, somewhere, deep, deep down; yet one can bear to touch the bottom. But when loving anyone carries one away, one goes down deeper and deeper, and yet feels that there is a fathomless gulf beyond."